K Moshe, born as a child with no dreams of only chasing dragonflies and watching trains passing by. She was born in a town in the north of Iraq. She travelled to England to study and found herself stranded as her country of birth was in war with the Britain and the West. Now she is a mother, a woman with a different accent and with a story to tell. In her first debut book, she has captured the life experience of a lost generation of Iraq, torn by wars and scared by its aftermath. At present, she lives in a town in Scotland.

This book is dedicated to you, my reader, and to Him who made you precious in His sight.

K Moshe

AND THEN HE SHOWED UP

AUSTIN MACAULEY PUBLISHERS™

LONDON • CAMBRIDGE • NEW YORK • SHARJAH

A CIP catalogue record for this title is available from the British Library.

ISBN 9781398414532 (Paperback)
ISBN 9781398405851 (ePub e-book)

www.austinmacauley.com

First Published 2022
Austin Macauley Publishers Ltd®
1 Canada Square
Canary Wharf
London
E14 5AA

My thanks to my readers who gave me the reason to write this book. Thanks also to every person whose path crossed mine. Each one of them shaped my existence in ways they may never know. Writing this book has been an intense encounter but with a healing touch. And finally my eternal gratitude to my family and my Maker, my all in all.

Preface

I was less than an ordinary little girl, not much different from any other little girl in my neighbourhood; thin and malnourished-looking. Everything I owned was a hand-me-down: any new piece of clothing I wore was a product of my big sister's creative mind and hands, with a clip here and a cut there. By transforming my big brother's old trousers or shirt, she fashioned a brand-new item of clothing, one which I could use. She had the pleasure of cutting my hair too – not always to my liking, though – especially when the haircut made me look like a little boy. I grew up and became a young lady, still wearing hand-me-downs, but now with long, beautiful hair. I fell in love with a handsome, rich young man who was everything I wasn't and had everything I didn't. Marrying him was, and still is, a question; his dad, today in his eighties, shakes his head from side to side, trying to figure out: why did he agree for his oldest son to marry someone like me?

I went through labour three times. I lived in various addresses and took up various jobs along the way as many other women would do. Today, I am still living, like many other middle-aged women are. Therefore, you may question the purpose of reading further. I would humbly express that I believe my life has been anything but an ordinary one. I experienced situations that tested the little confidence I had in myself to the extreme. I witnessed existence that exhibited and transformed what was a miserable being into a triumphant leap only because He showed up every time; I cried out to Him loudly or silently. Is my life worth writing about? Is it worth you reading about? Yes, and forgive me for wasting your time if you think otherwise.

Introduction

Early morning on a Friday, the weekday we all look forward to, I was getting ready to go to work. The phone rang. It was my brother. 'She is gone.'

My brain forgot how to process the words which followed after. I had to excuse myself and end the call. Although I knew her death was only a matter of time, as the last two months of her life were too hard to bear. What my brother uttered were just words, but their impact started the eruption of a volcano inside, then extended to shatter the world around me.

I went to work that day like a robot. Nothing was registering emotionally. Like a robot, I performed the necessary motions of the day. I did not say a word to anybody at work. I delivered the lessons. Throughout the day, there was another conversation taking place within my head. As if I had another mouth silently screaming in my students' faces, who were looking at me while I was in full flow delivering the lesson: 'Do you even realise what has happened today?'

I went home after work, and I told my family. I then went to my room, shutting the door and the world outside. I am unsure of how to describe the noises my body made: wailing, weeping, howling, or sobbing? They were noises that encompassed all of her pain and mine, all of her suffering and mine. A lifetime of miserable slow death. All of the creation surrounding me, reduced to naught; all I could see, hear, feel, and breathe was my precious mother. I was transported back to the courtyard of my childhood family home. My mother and I, sitting on the floor, with figures of farm animals, made for me from clay and my tears flowing, as though they were a part of this scene.

Chapter 1

When I Belonged

My parents couldn't read or write, but they both ensured that all of their children had university qualifications. My mother used to say: 'If you have an education, you will be able to support yourself financially. If anything goes wrong between you and your husband, you can always rely on your own income to live comfortably.' We didn't have much, but we had enough. My parents were immigrants who fled the persecutions of Christian families living in the south of Turkey during the First World War under the Ottoman Empire. They were faced with three options: renounce your faith, leave your home, or execution. They had to leave all their wealth behind and start again. They settled in one of the villages in the north of Iraq. All of the residents of the village were Christians. Their faith had survived many centuries, since when the early disciples were sent to Iraq. My parents spoke Aramaic, the ancient language which Jesus had spoken. Arabic was their third language, after Kurdish. Until their final days with us, my parents couldn't speak Arabic very well.

My parents were loving, and the little they could produce was received with gratitude by my six siblings and me. We never complained. My father worked as a chef assistant in a hotel which was linked to the railway station in our small town. He was good at what he did. Occasionally, he would let us try his creations. Of course, we wouldn't have the luxury ingredients they acquired at the hotel, but whatever my father came up with tasted delicious. My parents' relationship was warm. What I watched and experienced as a child pleased me. They would do house chores together, which I figured was a sign of a loving relationship. My mum had her own version of a washing machine. In those days, there were no washing machines, tumble dryers, and dishwashers – the esteemed occupants of my kitchen today. No, my mum's washing machine was a big round deep object which she called a Tashta. It was made of some sort of metal, probably tough aluminium, and was over a metre wide in diameter and less than a foot in depth. She would sit in our courtyard on her Takhta, which was a very low handmade wooden seat. She would wash the clothes with washing powder and hand them to my dad. He would sit next to her, on his Takhta, with his Tashta in front of him, running the rinsing cycle. My dad could squeeze out more water from the washed clothes than my mum. When the two Tashta weren't acting as washing machines, they became our swimming pools, a source of fun for us kids. The drying lines were in the courtyard. As children, we knew how hard our parents worked to have the clothes cleaned, so we never needed anyone to tell us not to go near the washing lines.

The main train station was half a mile away from my house. There were so many railway lines and all sorts of trains passing by my house, black and green. The steam engines looked like big, noisy monsters. Thick smoke plumed from their chimneys and near the wheels, billowing around the vehicle as it moved slowly. Every time, they would fill the front of my house with hot smoke. The noises they made as they chugged out of the station still rings in my ears. It would start really slowly as if it needed us to go behind it and give it a push. But it would accelerate and get noisier by the time it passed my house. My little friends and I would line up against the fence erected in front of our houses, waving franticly and shouting out loud 'bye bye bye', until the last carriage passed by my house. The train driver always sounded the horn as the train approached my house. We used to think he is saying 'bye bye' back to us, obviously not. My mum didn't want the washing to be hanging out when these engines and their smoke were parading. The washing would need to be gathered, folded and stored away before we could hear the evening trains leaving the station.

We used to eat homemade bread, the outcome of another joint effort by my parents. My mum would start the process until the little circular-shaped dough was ready to cook. They were called Takherta. Dad would take the trays of the freshly made little circles of dough outside where the Tanoora was. Tanoora is like an outdoor handmade oven. It was made of clay, not quite round shaped, but wider at the bottom, with a round opening at the top. The Tanoora was powered by wood. So far, my reader, you have learnt your first four words in Aramaic. All the four begin with the letter T. There was a very large olive tree at the front of my house, near the Tanoora, which I used to climb on a daily basis. I spent many hours up at the top watching what lay beyond the railway lines, houses, streets and other spaces which my little height wouldn't allow me to see if I was standing on the ground. The olive tree produced much-loved olives. Harvest times were more than once a year. When the olives were ripe, there would be thousands of little green, red, or black depending on how much sunshine they had enjoyed. My favourite part was to sit under the tree, head down and hands on my head, while my dad gave the branches a good shake. It rained olives on me. They looked like and felt like little stones, but I wasn't hurt. At times, I would hide on top of the tree when I was a child in a bad mood or when I didn't want to see anyone, and I didn't want anyone to see me.

My mum was what every mother should be, loving and full of goodness. She was very creative in every way. Although she couldn't read me bedtime stories, as she was illiterate, she would tell me many stories until I fell asleep. She knew most of Disney stories even before I knew Disney existed. Every night, she would repeat the three little pigs, little red riding hood, the billy goats and many more, ones which even Disney haven't heard of yet.

One of the most precious times of my childhood with my mother was when she used to make small animal figurines from clay for me. She would use the red clay that Dad and I would go and dig up from the outskirts of my town. My mum would shape the wet clay into an outline of various farm animals, which I asked for. Once we both agreed on the shape and the size, she would leave them in the sun to dry. I loved my little animals. They were so easy to mend when an ear or a tail broke off.

We didn't have prams in those days, so when we went out, my mother would carry my youngest sister, and my dad always carried me until I was strong enough to walk on my own. Materially, we didn't have much, but our home was filled with love for each other and filled with faith in God, which was vividly evident in our daily lives.

My house had a big courtyard in the middle, which was surrounded by all the rooms and the stairs which took us to the roof terrace. The courtyard was our play area. The flooring was made of hard concrete, except for a small squared island where a huge eucalyptus tree was planted. I didn't like the concrete much, especially during summer. The heat of the day would cause the concrete to become a burning flat surface on which you could cook an egg on. We used to get our feet burnt if we dared to forget to wear our shoes. As with the same speed you went out to the courtyard, you would dart back into the room even faster, tiptoeing with burnt toes.

Since my childhood, I was aware of God's presence in seen and in unseen ways. My first appreciation of His creation happened when I was three or four years old. One day, it started to snow. Until that day, I had never seen snow before. My mum might have mentioned it in one of her bedtime stories, but I did not know how the snow looked or how it felt when touched. I went out to the courtyard and saw the snow falling. Everywhere was covered in white, the tree, the floor and even the washing lines – all covered in white, including me. I loved it. I was mesmerised by its magical effects, and it made me so happy. I did not know what was going on. I kept running continuously to the room where my siblings had congregated and out back to the courtyard like an idiot telling everybody as if nobody else had noticed these marvellous and mysterious white cold flakes. I was shouting on top of my voice, so everybody could hear me, including the neighbours on both sides of our terraced house. 'There is flour everywhere. There is flour everywhere!'

When I was probably five years old, on Easter Sunday, my father gave me what was equivalent to two ten pence coins. This was a very memorable day as getting two coins was not a regular thing. As with every Sunday, we walked to Church, which was half an hour journey. At an early age, I perceived the church as the house of God, and everything inside it belonged to Him. I had a plan for the two ten pence coins. One of them was for me to keep, and the other one was for God to keep. I was going to put the one for God in the collection tray. In the row behind us sat one of my teachers with her family. She had a little girl who was probably my age. Having the mother of a family as a teacher made the family rich. They even had a nice light blue car. Their clothes looked so different from mine. During the service, I was too focused on the two coins. I was holding them so tightly in my hand. Still, I managed to drop one of them on the floor. It rolled away behind me in the direction where the girl was sitting. Half of my fortune was gone. I stayed on my seat, and I didn't run after the rolling coin, but I desperately hoped an adult would tell me to go and get it. A voice in my little head scolded me, 'You are in the house of God; the coin which fell on the floor now belongs to God.' The coin was left where it rolled to, no objection here. Soon the other coin ended up in the collection tray. Whatever plan I had for my coin, after the church service, it didn't come to pass. I had a grumpy face and petted lip for the rest of the day. However, what annoyed me most happened at the end of the service. As we got up to leave, I saw my teacher's daughter bent down and picked my coin. She then very quickly put it in her pocket. I was shocked, so I stood there like an inanimate object. I didn't say anything, but obviously, the scene made me mad for days. For months I had stopped liking that teacher. I would say in my head, 'Why didn't she tell her daughter to give me back my coin?' Every time I saw the teacher, I would see my coin instead.

My mum knitted our jumpers, and the younger siblings enjoyed the many hand-me-down items from the older ones, and so the wheel of life continued. I would've been still in primary school when my older sisters were proper teenagers. Being ten years old, I would be longing to inherit any item from my big sisters, not sure about shoes, though. Unfortunately, their shoes did not fit me very well as my feet were much smaller than the size of the newly acquired shoes. Still, who was I to complain? Everything was gladly received. It was a memorable day when I finally got to inherit the black pair of boots with crisscross laces at the front. Years before, these boots belonged to my older sister, and years prior to that, these treasured boots belonged to my oldest sister. I had thin legs, and having been bequeathed my older sister's boots, I couldn't keep the dreaded boots up. No matter what I did or how tight I pulled the laces together, they wouldn't stay up. They looked so ugly on me. 'Why aren't my legs fuller and fatter, so the boots won't drag down?' I moaned to myself. For days, I kept the boots under my bed, and when there was nobody around, I would put them on and walk with them on, pacing across the room. I had to bend down to try and hold the side brim of the boots with my hand to keep the boots up. And one day, my eyes lit with delight, and my face was painted with an anticipated excitement as a thought came to my little head. Why don't I keep my pyjama trousers on and pull my tight on top of it! So, I took my socks off and put my tights on at a pace I haven't done before. I pulled my tights over my pyjama trousers very anxiously with my mind racing faster than my hands were acting to find out if this amazing idea would work. My legs became fatter, but they didn't look very even. I tried smoothing the creases of my pyjama trousers under the tights, shoving them this direction and that direction. I was discussing with myself while I was fixing the bumpy bits telling myself this will be hidden inside the boots, so no one is going to notice it. The newly created padding inside the boots worked. Yes, it worked, and I was over the moon. And so, I wore the boots every day till the holes in the soles couldn't be mended by my father any longer.

The house we lived in was part of a housing scheme which belonged to the railway establishment. All the fathers in my neighbourhood worked in the railway station. There were probably less than seven terraced houses, all facing the railway lines. There was a very high chain-link fence erected in front of our houses as a safety measure. At the end of the terraced houses was a heavy metal gate. I could only open it if I used both my hands. There were so many railway lines parallel to each other. Some of them had train carriages parked on. My little friends and I used to play inside the parked carriages. We would climb up the not so comfortable thin and short steel stepladder. Once inside, we would play any game we wanted. We played tag and houses and pretended to be passengers waving to the imaginary people lined up on the station waving back.

Freight trains would pass by my house too. Some of these trains used to carry minerals, a mixture of yellow powder and small broken rocks, sulphur, I think. Once the train was away, we would run and collect any droppings on the side of the railway lines. One of these powders, the grey one, was our favourite. It was fun to play with. As kids, we had no idea, of course, what the powders we were touching were. Except they were our magic, our secret, and a fun ingredient for much-anticipated experiments. We would make a hole in the ground, put the powder in the hole, pour cold water over it and pock it with a stick. We would wait and watch. In no time, bubbles and more bubbles would develop and rise. This was it. Bubbles rose and burst. Moments later, the whole area was filled with an unpleasant smell. We would start giggling as if we produced those smells. We were dealing with mysterious potions, and we were chuffed with our great discovery. Fun was over when the bubbles became flat. Off we were to catch dragonflies or to attempt capturing bees. This required special skills and precision. Dragonflies were in different colours, and they were easier to capture. All we had to do was to bring the two sets of wings together and press hard with our little thumb and index finger. My friends and I would be quiet once we spotted our prey. The bee had to be resting on a big flower with big and wide petals. We would sneak quietly and slowly to approach the flower. And when the moment was right, we would quickly gather and all the petals together and hold their ends tightly. The bee would go mad inside its prison. We would only hold the petals for a minute or two, and then we would let go, throwing the flower and what was inside it as far away as possible from us, and run for our lives, hoping the bee didn't identify us as the captures. We were kids with no care in the world. In our little minds, we had done nothing wrong. The danger we put ourselves in terrifies me. What if the minerals were harmful to the skin? What if one of the train carriages started moving while we were inside? Of course, our parents were oblivious to what we were up to during the long afternoon hours.

Each year, from probably the month of March till September, we would sleep on the roof terrace at night-time. A priceless experience to behold. We would hang mosquito net using four poles on each corner of the bed. When fitted on top of the bed, the net looked like a white rectangular box. The bottom hems of the net would be tucked under the mattress. My sister Magdalene's bed was next to mine as we shared a big net. It was our own little house. Magdalene was nine years older than me, but we were best friends. The nets were see-through, and they were made of very thin cotton. During the night, the sky was lit with millions of stars. Some bigger and brighter than others. Because of these beautiful diamonds like stars, the sky had a rich navy-blue colour. Many a night, I would see shooting stars so frequently. By the time I caught sight of one on this side of the sky, I could've missed others. Early in the morning, there would be lots of eucalyptus leaves on top of the net. It gave me joy in clearing these leaves. So, I would be lying on my back, and I would kick one of my legs as high as I could to flick the leaves off the net, the roof of our little house. Some of these leaves were harder to shift as they needed more than one kick to send them off to the floor. At times, I would end up sitting up to get rid of the leaves with my hand.

Our next-door neighbour had many children. Each child with a similar age to mine or one of my siblings. The one who was my age, my childhood friend, had the nickname Choona. In order to get to my house, I had to pass by Choona's house. The only problem was my friend's family kept chickens and one sheep, how? Who knows? They had a huge white cockerel, which scared me to death. We called him a double cake. Why double cake? I was only five or six years old when this good for nothing animal took it upon itself to make my life miserable. Every time it noticed me, this stupid ugly thing would run fast towards me. Screaming or not, it didn't make any difference. It kept charging, flying up and nipping my bottom. I hated my life, and I hated double shit even more. I hated how it moved, leaning so heavily on each side as if it was going to touch the ground. I still hate it even today. I wished it dead. Years later, when my friend's family moved to another city, the awful creature – who was still alive – departed with them.

The sheep, however, was a different story. It was big, smelly and placid. The sheep was our big pet. Choona and I would love it when her mother would say, 'The sheep must be hungry. Come on, take the sheep out, and feed it.' We would go out in the neighbourhood, strolling for hours looking for a Mulberry tree. Their leaves were the sheep's favourite food. We were little and thin, and the sheep was much bigger than us, but being sheep, we could manage it, unlike the monster double cake. We would walk in the neighbourhood for hours with the sheep as a prominent member of our company. Being a sheep, it did not know when and where to let go of its poo. It was then that we would walk alongside it, giving the sheep some privacy to do its business. Of course, it created a mess. The mess was in the form of tiny little dark green brownish and dry balls. The sheep would produce these balls and would drop them randomly everywhere. We never cleared the mess our pet left behind. We didn't know we were doing anything wrong. Every time the sheep made the baabaa sound, we would join in like idiots. I am not sure if we were pretending to be sheep or letting the sheep know it was one of us. One day, and as we didn't know any better, we fed the sheep bread, thinking we were giving it a special treat. In the evening, the sheep became really ill. It was lying on the floor of the courtyard on its side, making sad noises. Its eyes were closing slowly; then, with much effort, the sheep would try to open them. The sheep nearly died, and I was sent home. Choona's mum's face was straight, and that night I didn't hear her familiar words as I left: 'Say hello to your mum.' These were always her final words when it was time for me to go home. Choona didn't come to the door with me. Choona and I had the look of a confused and terrified child on our faces. A lesson was learnt: sheep and bread don't mix. I was glad and relieved as our pet didn't die that night. However, we were not allowed to take it out again. The sheep was entrusted to our older siblings.

Chapter 2

Brick by Brick

Being an employee of the railway industry, my dad was given the opportunity to buy a plot of land with a much-reduced price, and in any town he wanted. He chose to buy one in the capital. My dad retired from work when I was twelve years old. It was a big change for everybody. Starting a new school halfway through the term was very stressful. My older siblings were nearing the age of applying to university courses. The university in the capital offered the best quality of education, and it offered courses in a wider range of disciplines. My father didn't stop working after his retirement. Once we settled in the capital, my dad was looking for a job. He continued earning money until he was in his seventies.

Moving house was a big upheaval, but the change enriched my parents' life as we had many relatives living in the capital, including my mum's only brother and my dad's only living brother. We stayed temporarily in three different rented accommodations before we managed to own our first and last house. Each rented accommodation had a story of hardship as it was shared with another family. We struggled big-time with space, or more precisely, the lack of it, but we built rich relationships with the other families. Overcoming the experience of living as tenants sharing the same house with another family was achieved with a little bit of sacrifice and tolerance. It was a type of living many people today wouldn't survive for one day. Having lived through these times made us appreciate having our own space. The house my parents built had two rooms, a kitchen and a bathroom. It was a huge milestone, especially for my mum. It was her own palace, for her family to enjoy, not sharing it with other families, and no landlord lording it over her.

Unlike how life is today, if you wanted to buy a house, you would go to the bank and get a mortgage. Perhaps the bank would offer you a loan for the full price of the house. If not, then probably for most of it. This wasn't the case for my parents. We didn't even know banks existed. In order to build a house, you had to have the money in cash. My parents had to borrow money from relatives who were willing to part with their cash. My mother had to ask so many of my big cousins and distant relatives for money. I used to tag along with her during these visits, like her shadow. While I was writing this line, I remembered scenes from Charlie Chaplin's black and white silent movie *The Kid*. I am not sure why I didn't throw stones at any windows, and my mum didn't offer to fix them in order to make money. Perhaps it was the sight of my mum and me, an adult and a child on the move, tasked with a great mission, collecting money. My mum was highly esteemed by our relatives. She was sincere, kind and she commanded respect and love from everybody who knew her. So, with every visit, my mum would come home with a bit more money in her purse. With every amount of money collected, a few more rows of bricks would be added to our house.

While our house was getting slowly built, my mum would pay the building site a visit almost every day. She loved standing within the borders of her land. For her, it was like being in heaven. To get there, she would catch a bus, then she would walk for a few miles, in the heat of the day. There weren't many houses built in the neighbourhood yet, but they had started to appear here and there. I can truly say my mother witnessed the rise of the house with each row of bricks that went up. The house meant the world to my mother.

This house meant the world to me too. I was much older now. I had experienced rapid changes in my sibling's lives. My life was enriched by having many siblings, but throughout life, I had a closer relationship with Magdalene. My heart and mind are filled with fond memories of her input in my childhood. She would ensure I did my homework, and while she was studying, I would sit beside her and learn what she was studying. To this day, at times, while chatting on the phone, we would laugh while reciting the poems that we both memorised together for her Arabic language subject. She had to do it to pass her exams, and I had to learn it just because of her. Magdalene was like my nanny, and in later years, she became my agony aunt. By now, my two oldest sisters had graduated, and they were married and working. One of them worked as a primary school teacher, and Magdalene was a Maths teacher. My other sister was going through her final year in medical school. My brother was a third-year university student studying for an Engineering degree. And I was sitting my National Baccalaureate exams. Every weekend my big sister would come, with her young children, to visit my parents' house. As the house increased in the number of its occupants at the weekends, it also increased in size. At a later date, two more rooms were added at the front of the house. Each brick of the house was injected with the joyous hustle and bustle sounds of family gatherings. At times, we would be all sitting in the front garden, chatting away, and my mum would be the one who happily prepared the food and served it. And in between, trays of cups of tea would arrive unannounced.

My parents saw the house as their own castle. It wasn't the bricks and mortars, but as my dad used to say, 'This is a blessed house.' My parents witnessed the weddings and the graduations of their children while living in that house. Life was good. No war and no soldiers everywhere yet. My parents were enjoying the fruit of their labour. We even bought a television, in colour no less. My parents would be watching a program or a drama, and as they both couldn't speak Arabic very well, they wouldn't have a clue what was going on. They would take a turn to ask whoever was in the room. 'What did this character say or what did this other character reply?' It was so funny to watch and listen to. My dad's words were: 'Da mo deele mara?' Few more new words in Aramaic for you, my reader. This time it is a whole new sentence. Which basically means 'What is he/she saying?' Magdalene, who was the patient one, would always explain every scene of the program or the movie. It was a harder task for her if the movie was in English or in any other language. My sister would have to read the subtitles in Arabic first, and then she would translate the text into Aramaic. At times, and before Magdalene would have the chance to get the words out, my dad would contribute by guessing what the character was saying. Very rarely, he would guess the events or the plot correctly. My mum, on the other hand, didn't waste her

28

breath. She would wait to hear the scene translated. If my parents were watching a film on their own, the movie would for sure have a totally different storyline. It would be the one my parents made up.

Good times didn't last long. Iran and Iraq war started. It was an eight long year war (September 1980 till August 1988). Hundreds of types of weapons were used, supplied by well over twenty countries. The result was the death of nearly a million lives, including those not counted for. Because of this war, there were over four hundred new companies created in one country alone to supply war-related products. To some countries, the war was an opportunity to creating new jobs and generating prosperity, but to the countries at war, it was the path to death. My older brother was called to join the Army. At the end of each of his brief leaves, I would wake up early morning with my mum to see him off. The thought of this could have been his last visit ever never crossed my mind. The main content of his sack was homemade hard cakes, stuffed with walnuts and sugar, which were essential to sustain him when food couldn't reach him at the front. It was always pitch-black outside when my brother left to go to the front. Every time we said goodbye to him, my last words were 'Alaha minookh khoni'. Which translates to 'May God be with you, my brother'.

Magdalene had her first and only daughter by now. Unfortunately, soon after, Magdalene's husband was captured as a prisoner of war. He was tormented with a 'death mixed with life' kind of living where he was for eight and a half long years, and she was suffering in so many different ways, hundreds of miles away from him. Magdalene would spend a few days of the week living at my parents' house and the rest of the week with her in-laws. Only Magdalene's Maker knows what kind of hardship she endured during these years. My father had a soft spot for my niece. A very special bond between the two of them started, and it continued until my father's last breath. My father enjoyed walking, and so when my niece's little legs were strong enough to walk, my father would take her to the local shops. At times they would reward themselves with an ice lolly, just for the two of them. They would make sure it was all consumed, and their lips were wiped clean before they were back home. No traces of guilty pleasure were left. When it came to ice cream and ice lollies, everybody in my family wanted one, and they should not be exclusive to the oldest and the youngest family members. A few years later, as my little niece started school, she would be holding my father's hand, and off they went. He would drop her off at the gate of the nursery, and a few hours later, he would be back waiting to pick her up. At times, you would hear my dad singing to my niece during daily walks. When her speaking voice became clearer, she would join in singing along, although more often for when she knew the words. It was then when her voice would drown his. Many of these songs would've been from my fathers' childhood, his own version of nursery rhymes. My father never spoke about his life in the south of Turkey. The only thing I have heard him say was he would go swimming in a loch called Vat. My niece used to call my dad 'babby sawa', which means 'my old father'.

The special bond between the two of them continued during the following years. Things about my dad, which annoyed all of us, to my niece they did not exist. When she used to get her homework marked, or she would receive the results of any exam, it was my father she ran to first, jumping up and down with every praise he bestowed upon her. As my niece grew older, she had the most amazing warm and soulful singing voice. This, of course, meant my father was getting older, so did his voice. It was her turn then to sing for him. During the following years, she mentally constructed a list of his favourite songs. And during the last few months of my father's life, my niece would sit on his side, and with her soothing singing voice, she would feed his soul. His own little nightingale was singing the songs he taught her, but his weak body wouldn't enable him to join in, only listening.

My brother-in-law was one of the lucky prisoners of war to be released. He made it back home, but many thousands and thousands of others never returned. Each one of them had a tragic tale stamped on their forehead. By now, my brother-in-law was a total stranger to his daughter. A year or two later, Magdalene had a son. Magdalene still lives with her husband today; however, their life is a story for another book. A life summed up as damaged goods. War damaged, no less. If people were given the title of a "saint" while alive, Magdalene should be the first one to get it. My niece would be the next on the list for the "little saint" title. Magdalene was twenty-seven years old when the war alienated her husband from her life. Magdalene's life was never the same again. Wars damage the country as a whole. But they damage individuals from the inside. Even though people think war might be over, but the brokenness of an individual's inmost being could never be repaired. My brother-in-law never spoke about the eight and a half long years of his youth, which the war burnt, but we all witnessed its impact on the rest of his years and on the life of his little family.

Chapter 3

He Is Their Brother

Years after moving to the capital, I was thrilled to find out my childhood neighbour and friend Choona, my fellow shepherdess, had moved to the capital too. Her family lived at a ten-minute walk from my house. What joy? So, our friendship rekindled and continued for the following years, no cockerel this time. We grew up together, and by now, we were teenagers. Her family was like my extended family. I would go to her house many times a week. Choona shared a room with three of her sisters. There were four single beds in their room and a two-door wardrobe to share. The wardrobe had a small mirror. At times the five of us would be crowding around the little mirror when trying to put makeup on. And if it happened to be a cold day, Choona and her sisters would be still in bed. Nice and cosy tucked under their covers. I needed no invitation. I would choose a spot and sit at the end of one of the beds and extend the cover over my legs. We would gab for hours. If they had something to eat, and I would join in; no invitation here either. Choona and I went to the same secondary school, and we went to the same church.

Every time I left the house, I had to pray and ask God to keep the stray dogs away from my path. In fact, we had a little song/prayer we used to recite. Its words were 'Shemon Kepa, kiple el kepa, Maran rekheshlae, etheh shishle, kalba wishle, bdokeh pishle, lapish nasha quad gargeshle'. This time, my reader, a whole prayer in Aramaic. It translates to 'Simon the rock, bent down to pick a stone, the Lord passed by, he shook His hand, the dog dried out, stayed on its spot, no person around to drag the dog away'.

Very few dogs were kept as pets in those days. Dogs roamed the streets like kings. They were scary things, especially if there was a pack of them coming towards you. If I saw the dogs from a distance, I would return home instead. I never took a chance with wild dogs. If, however, there were other people around, and they were heading in the same direction as mine, I would walk behind them. If a dog approached us, one of the guys would throw a stone or two to scare it away. I never wanted to try it myself when alone, in case the dogs didn't take notice of me or they were not scared off by my stone. I would hate to think what could happen next as I am not a fast runner. Dogs scared me even more at night-time. If I was woken up by their barking, I would say to myself, 'There must be a burglar in the street.' I used to think, *Why would anyone be out in the streets in the middle of the night unless he was up to no good?* Dogs and burglars scared me and burdened my weary mind at night. The fear of having the two of them in my street caused me to freeze in my bed. I would listen intently to find out when the barking would stop or if the dogs hopefully started moving away from my street. I would try to fall asleep again. If the dogs didn't go away, and if I had the courage to move, I would dart to my mum's bed.

Unfortunately, evil was lurking in the neighbourhood. The damage it caused stayed with me for many years. The memories of what happened on one dark day stirred my emotions in a sickly way, but outwardly I was motionless. My mind rejected what was a reality. It was two worlds colliding in front of me, the one filled with love and care I experienced inside my house. The other contrast inside my next-door neighbour's house. The world then, compared to the world I live in today. I am sure similar incidents are still happening today. They happen in various parts of the world. They mark the absence of love and forgiveness.

Our next-door neighbour ran a small shop. The neighbours were not Christians; we had different values and principles to theirs, especially considering how girls and women were treated. But my family lived in a harmonious way with all of our neighbours. Nothing to complain about. My neighbour had two daughters, aged seventeen and eighteen, and a son who was a bit older. The girls didn't go to school, and therefore they were in the house most of the time. Their parents would accompany them for any outing. Many of these would be for visiting their relatives or going shopping.

I am not sure what the two girls thought of life, knowing the kind of existence they lived. In those days, there was a big shortage of labour, and so there were lots of Egyptian workers who took up all sorts of jobs. They would come and work for a number of years, save some money, and then go back home. This happened to be the start of the end of the two sisters. Apparently, the older sister had met an Egyptian young man, and consequently, they fell in love. This Egyptian young man was not her cousin, of course, so how did she dare to choose

34

someone else to fall in love with but her cousin. Their custom was a young girl's first choice for marriage had to be her cousin. Only when the cousin doesn't concur, only then she could get another man picked for her by her family. Of course, it didn't matter how old or young the cousin was, married or not; this was not an issue. If the cousin was married and he wanted her, then she became his second wife. Falling in love with an Egyptian young man was seen as an act of defiance. It was totally unforgivable. It brought shame, not to the parents alone, but to the whole clan. The girl who was in love, foolishly and naively, had decided to leave her parents' house and move in with the young man. Her sister, even more foolishly and naively, accompanied her.

Our house had a high-walled fence. It had a white painted sheet of a heavy metal front gate, which was as tall as the wall. You couldn't see what was happening in the street unless you opened the front gate. On one dreadful morning, I left home to go to university. As I opened the front gate, it wasn't the dogs which concerned me this time; instead, it was a far more sinister disturbance. I saw police cars and ambulance vans right in front of my house. My heart jumped. This was the first time I had seen so many emergency cars, all in one place and so close to me. I am not a curious person or one with an inquisitive nature. I didn't even have the courage to ask what was going on. I continued walking to the main road to catch the bus. I came back home in the evening and learnt what caused the commotion in the morning. It was far worse than any imaginable scenario. Evil struck and took the lives of two young ladies. To make the matter worse, the two young sisters were shot by their brother. You might say: 'What? Is this real?' Unfortunately, it was.

As the girls stayed with the Egyptian boyfriend, the parents were compelled and pressured by their relatives to avert the crisis. Their uncle had contacted the girls with the false pretence of aiming for a reconciliation with their parents. The girls didn't want to fall out with their parents, and they didn't want to be cut off by their extended family, so they agreed to whatever lies their uncle told them. In the meantime, the uncle notified the parents about his effort to bring the girls back home. The uncle proved to be a snake. The twisted, evil-minded uncle had smooth-talked the girls into their grave. The parents were cornered. Weeks later, we learnt that the uncle had said to the parents, 'I have got them back, so what are you going to do with them?' The two sisters were promised forgiveness. Instead, their uncle took them back home only to have them killed. Their death was regarded as an honour killing. The brother got six months in prison, and soon he was out, a free-living man. He didn't even serve the six months. The two sisters had their lives terminated, dead in the grave for real and forever. They didn't even get many people attending their funeral. Perhaps a few neighbours, those who were remembering their own dead and not moaning the death of the two young sisters.

The uncle never entered my neighbour's house again; neither did any of their relatives. Even though the girls' lives were cut so short, the parents were still cast out by the extended family. I know I am not to judge other people, but I couldn't help feel for these girls who were only a year or two younger than me. How is this allowed? How can a family be cursed with such a horrible culture which, for stupid and useless values, allowed to destroy the lives of their own girls? These cruel values were made to be more important than life.

Where was love? Love sounds like a simple concept to many of us but, unfortunately, not then. What if? What if these two girls were born to different parents? To my parents? If only they were born in a different country, they would've been still alive, breathing, enjoying life, not discarded bones in their grave.

My father would go to my next-door neighbour's shop and sit with the parents for a long time. My father was like their angel, their counsellor, and simply a father who truly felt their pain. By befriending them, my father gave them an opportunity to pour out their grief, which otherwise would have drowned them from the inside. I also admired my father for reaching out to the devastated parents who, by losing their girls, lost everything. To them, my father was the only goodness in their lives. God used my father in ways none of us could underestimate.

Chapter 4

What the Bridge Witnessed

When it was time for me to go to university, I managed to get the grades that would've allowed me to choose any course I wanted. Looking back now, I think I was ill-informed. And like many 17- or 18-year-old students today, I didn't choose my course wisely. When I was in secondary school, I was my brother's manual photocopier. He was at university doing an Engineering course. Whenever he missed a lecture, my brother would make me copy the notes of a friend of his. In doing so, I had the opportunity to find out about the content of his course. I thought I liked the subjects covered. There were lots of Maths, Drilling, Production, Well logging and Secondary Recovery, etc. I was wrong. So foolishly, I applied to do a BSc Hons in Petroleum Engineering, the same course as my brother's. I became a first-year university student while my brother was in his final year.

My brother and I, and on certain days would catch the same buses. Some of our lecture theatres and labs were situated in the same building. Bumping into my brother from time to time during the day helped make the transition to university life much bearable for me. My surroundings were like an extension to our home just because he was there. Soon his friends started saying hello to me. My brother was never impressed at all. Having me around at home was more than enough; extending it to his surrounding at university was getting too much for him. Being like his shadow at university kind of spoiled his day. There was only one other female student on my course in a class of seventy. She had a sister, who was a third-year Chemical Engineering student. Earlier in the year, the other female fellow student would disappear after the lectures and join her big sister's group. During the breaks, I ended up standing on my own, a few metres away from where my brother was. He would be surrounded by a circle of his friends. Being final year students, my brother and his friends owned the place. The stern faces the lecturers exhibited while teaching me would transform; instead, they would put on smiley faces when stopping to chat with my brother and his friends. Somehow, this made me feel so good and important; hoped these lecturers would know he is my brother. Yet, I was this little skinny girl standing there like a scarecrow facing my brother to scare him. One day my brother had had enough. He waited till we got home, then he said to me in a harsh manner, shouting and pointing the finger at me: 'Why do you have to stand there facing me? Could you not find somewhere else to stand? Why do you have to embarrass me like this?' I went quiet, head down. He didn't appreciate the little self-esteem I tried hard to build up was only arising from seeing him nearby. It made me belong to the place since he was there. I kept those thoughts to myself.

I replied in a shaky and soft voice with my head still down, 'Sorry.' I went to another room feeling let down.

I wasn't very enthusiastic about my course; however, I plodded along and hoped for the best. You don't drop out, no, you just carry on. I am not sure if I enjoyed any part of it. I really didn't understand much of the topics covered. The lecturers in those days were set in their old-fashioned way of teaching. They acted as if they were Gods. We had one textbook and no other resources. How could I learn when nothing worked for me? I would come home, exhausted by the heat.

The bus journey to university was not an excuse, but honestly, it was a big factor for not enjoying university life. Getting inside a bus was such a huge achievement. I would wait for the bus forever. When it finally arrived, it was so full it didn't bother stopping to pick up more passengers. Some of these buses were articulated ones. It astounded me how the engine of those overloaded buses managed to pull the weight of the passengers. Although it never happened but I used to think, one day the two parts of this bus will come undone. Many times, I would walk in the wrong direction of where the bus should be taking me to in order to catch the bus further up the way. My daily journey to the university comprised of catching two different buses and a fifteen minutes' walk in between. You had to push your way through all these bodies; otherwise, you would be left behind. I hated being touched by men; many of them would do it on purpose. The fifteen minutes' walk between the two bus journeys led to a street where a big church building stood. From time to time, I would go inside the church and pray for a while before I continued my journey. The second bus would cross a bridge over the River Tigris and drop me off near the university buildings. At times, I would head straight to university bathrooms to clean my shoes, and the back of my lower legs as my tights would be covered with mud. Not all pavements were surfaced with tar, so we couldn't avoid walking on muddy areas. Some girls would put on a carrier bag on each foot on top of their shoes, a cheap version of wellington boots, in order to end up with clean shoes. Dogs, buses, and mud, and the day hadn't even started yet.

In my first year, I failed one of my subjects. All exam resits took place in September. I had all summer to revise. My resit exam was at 2:00 pm. I planned to go to the university's library early morning and spend several hours revising before the exam. I had to go over certain topics, which were a bit dry and difficult to memorise. As I was on my way to catch the second bus, I passed the church, and then I changed my mind and decided to go inside the church. I opened the church door and gasped. I am not sure what had happened there, but the inside of the church looked like a building site. There were dust and residue of cement and other building materials everywhere, on the floor, on the pews, and on the whole place. You could choke just by looking at it. You couldn't sit anywhere. I stood there and said to myself, 'The house of God should not look like this.' There was no way I could have left the building in that state. No discussion to be had.

Throughout my life, I have not been a fan of housework. I honestly am not good at it, and I certainly don't have the patience for it. My older and younger sisters were the opposite, so they had decided that the two of them would take charge of house chores; who was I to argue with that? Staring at the mess around me inside the church, a thought came to mind what if my two sisters were here now? They would've asked me to step aside, or even better, they would've asked me to go and wait outside. The two of them would've charged

41

like two machines without stopping until the whole place was pristine clean.

The priest's accommodation was on the upper floor, to the right-hand side of the building. I climbed the stairs and knocked on the door. The priest was in. He gladly agreed to my proposition with a smile on his face; I wasn't sure how to interpret. Did he wish good luck with a sarcastic tinge, or did he think I was an idiot? By now, I had totally forgotten about the exam, which was at 2:00 pm. I found out where the water supply was, the hose, the cleaning and dusting cloths. The floor of the church was tiled. There were far too many pews made of solid wood, so long and so heavy to move. They all had to be moved in order to clean the floor underneath. I had no idea where to start. However, all the pews were cleaned, the floor, all the surfaces, and what occupied them. The outside of the church was cleaned so were the stairs leading to the priest's accommodation. The place looked so clean; you were safe to breathe and a job well done, in my opinion. I stood there for a moment or two before I left with a satisfied smile on my face wondering where my strength came from. My clothes were drenched with water. I squeezed as much as I could out of my skirt and shook it a number of times. I am not sure what state I was in and what the passers-by thought of me, but I bet I looked amazing in my heavenly Father's sight. A beautiful thought filled me with content, and so I made it to the exam in time. I believe every question on the exam paper was handpicked by my Father above and probably answered by Him too. This time I didn't need to ask him in prayer. He saw, He gave, and I graciously received. I passed the exam with flying colours, and a second-year university student, lucky me!

Crowded buses, heat, lots of sweaty and bad-tempered people would cause me to walk the bus journey rather than wait for the bus. On one particular day, it was boiling hot as usual. The bus depot was so crowded. Every inch on the pavements was occupied by people. I sighed a hopeless sigh together with a hopeless thought as to how many buses would come and go before I could get inside one. As I hated fighting my way through the crowd and judging by the number of people around me waiting for the same bus, my feet took off and carried me away from the bus stop. So, I walked instead. It was a foolish thing to walk in the heat. My friend Choona's youngest sister had died from sunstroke one year on our first day back to school after the summer holiday. She was only six years old, and her death upset the old and the young at school and in the neighbourhood. Nonetheless, I walked. At times, you would see people holding their umbrellas up for a bit of shade. The walk led to a street which continued through the city centre. This was the main hub for shopping. The high-rise buildings on both sides of the roads offered a nice cool shaded area, a refuge from the burning sun. The main street in the city centre continued over a bridge on the River Tigris. The bridge was a beautiful piece of history. I was walking on the far side, away from the traffic. From time to time, I would glance at the muddy water, which was flowing so forcefully. Water scared me, rivers especially. Deep rivers with muddy water would drown me just by looking at them. I imagine the river as a powerful warrior with so many buried weapons lurking under the surface of the water. I, on the other hand, am a defenceless piece of fluff that would vanish with one look at this hypnotising enemy I fail to win over or convince to let go of me. These waters are an ongoing trigger to many nightmares I had to live through.

The incident which followed had left its mark on me and unsettled me for many years after. It happened so fast and so unexpected; my brain is still trying to work out why? I didn't choose to witness it. And I couldn't have avoided it. A few metres ahead of me, I saw a mother holding her toddler's hand. I notice life, and I get moved by it. I find it soothing to my soul when love and compassion are shown around me. As I was watching the mother and her child, I slowed my pace a bit to enjoy the scene. This was changed in a fraction of a second. A tall man passed by me. He was walking so fast and so close to me. He slightly brushed my left shoulder. He passed by me like a flash, so fast he could have tripped over or stumbled on the person in front of him. Something was not right about him, but I did not have time to figure it out. I did, however, notice his clothes were not fit to be seen anywhere. He was wearing what I could only describe as a ladies' nightdress with midi length. The dress looked old and dirty, and the hem was torn at parts. Perhaps it was never washed. He then moved to my right, heading towards the lady and her child. The child was on the inside, near the wall of the bridge. This man, with no thinking or feeling, like a zombie, picked the child up and, without any hesitation, lifted him over the bridge and dropped him down into the river!

The man continued walking at the same pace as if nothing happened. You could imagine the shock, the fear, and the disbelief which descended on the mother and on me. She started screaming on top of her voice. She was hitting her head and scratching her cheeks as if she was punishing herself for no fault of her own. Or probably she was releasing some of the pain's intensity through hurting herself. It felt like someone had turned the life off. I was in total shock and dismay. Scenes like this one don't even happen in the movies which I watch. If they were, then I would have switched the TV off and ran to another room. How do you prepare yourself for this? Why would any human being commit such an act of callous and utter depravity with no regard to a child's life whatsoever? Once again, I saw evil in charge, exhibiting its powers and destruction. It manifested itself in the action of one person and the total chaos which followed. The traffic stood still. People left their cars in the middle of the road and wandered around, wanting to know what was going on.

It was a long drop till the toddler reached the surface of the water. Tigris River was wide and deep. The water was flowing, fierce and too muddy to see anything through. To think my brother used to swim in this water as a teenager against my father's stern instructions not to go near it! My brother's guardian angel must have been swimming with him. Water is a ferocious power with no feelings; it does not know what to accept and what not. The river is not going to say, 'Oh no, a child is approaching, so we better bat it back to his mother where he belongs.' Water takes life and very rarely let's go of any. Death lives there, under the water, waiting for the next victim.

So, although evil was present, so were the heavenly beings. There was a man sitting inside his little fishing boat, probably waiting for the next fish to be caught, or probably he was fed up for not having caught anything yet. No matter how his day had started, I am sure the fisherman had never expected what came to him the next moment. He was right where the child was dropped. He instantly jumped in the water, not wasting one moment. The man disappeared into the muddy water for several minutes. Everybody was watching, with mixed emotions, not knowing what might happen next. Watching and holding our breath, but what an ending! The next thing we saw was the fisherman emerging from the water holding the child. The man put the child in his boat first, then he got into the boat himself and started moving towards the riverbank. So, it was now switched quickly to another set of feelings, the total opposite to what we were living through several minutes ago but just as intense. The mother had to run all the way to the end of the bridge, turn right and keep running to the bank of the river to claim her child back. There were no dry eyes. Everybody cheered and clapped and thanked God for the safety of both the child and the rescuer. I was exhausted with the rollercoaster of contrasting emotions. I wish I could say for every time the evil struck that its damage was controlled so swiftly like that day. Unfortunately, this is not always the case. That was the last time I walked over that bridge. The toddler was much lighter than me in weight, of course, but the troubled man was more than capable of lifting anybody instead. He knew exactly what he was doing. I imagine the event even now, so vividly, how he passed by me from my left-hand side, walked diagonally to get to the child, so calculated, so unexplainable, dropped the child in the river, as if nothing happened then swiftly continued his fast walk. Should I have waited for the bus and missed all this? Nobody knew what happened to the perpetrator. Did he move on to repeat his evil act somewhere else but differently? Was he ever caught? Who knows? Have you ever wondered what your angel have spared you from, today or yesterday?

Chapter 5

Father's Tears

I was 23 years old, a graduate with a BSc Hons in Engineering, living at home and unemployed. My grades weren't good enough to guarantee me a workplace in the capital, so I was offered a job in one of the oil fields near the borders of Iran. As the oil field was a short distance from a war front, my mother will not have it. I had to stay at home, unemployed. A friend of mine introduced me to a well-known artist who specialised in creating beautiful pieces of ceramics from clay imported from France. Her work was extraordinary. She would portray the history of Baghdad on Relief Sculpture, which protruded out of a flat surface of baked and coloured clay. Her work would end up adorning walls in various prestigious buildings in the city. She made her living from getting a commission or two a year. Watching her at work was the best lesson. She would let us play with clay and the tools she had to come up with our own creation. I spent three hours in her studio during weekdays. The only way I could describe this period of my life would be I was a free spirit, encapsulated in a world of my own. We used to make all sorts of home ornaments; beautiful ones, a commodity only the rich could afford to buy. They were made for those who knew where the studio was located. So, we had the regulars, always the rich and the sophisticated. We made such unique items; each one was a one of exquisite ashtrays and fruit bowls. What I enjoyed making most was a collection of small to medium-sized pieces of flat and free-formed shapes of ceramics with writings on coloured with various shades of greens, blues and reds. Those pieces were linked together, having chains of beads of various sizes dangling down at various positions and with different lengths. We would use metal wires and special pliers to cut and twist the wires into desired shapes after inserting a little bead. These pieces of beautifully designed and coloured ceramics would be connected to assemble a piece of art that would end up hanging on the walls of the homes of rich families or government buildings. Our customers loved them, and we loved making them. This life of "play with clay and colouring" suited my abstract random way of creating things. My mum's artistic mind would have been so fulfilled, and her pieces would've been outstanding.

I met Ray when I was a first-year university student. He was a friend of my brothers. Ray was everything that I wasn't, a handsome young man full of life and confidence. He was the oldest of five brothers. His father was a secondary school teacher and his mother, Miriam, was the headteacher for a local primary school. Being Christian and in Education, Ray's mum was one of few ladies in the city who reached her position. The majority of women her age could not read or write and never worked outside the house. She is lovely but authoritarian. She had successfully applied her managerial skills at home too. This served her well as it kept her five lively boys checked. Miriam was well respected, especially by the parents of hundreds of children she welcomed to her school every year. Being the oldest and clever at school, Ray was the pride of his parents. His dad would refer to him as the golden boy. In his opinion, no young girl was good enough for his son, let alone the insignificant me. As a family, they were well educated, wealthy and the envy of many people. I didn't know Ray very well, only through what my brothers would say about him by passing. When my brother was studying, Petroleum Engineering, Ray was studying Architecture. They would meet quite regularly at university. Occasionally Ray would come with my brother to our house. We attended the same church. Ray was loud, well-spoken, and so bold with his opinions, unlike me. He would start conversations and laugh and joke about people and situations. Everybody around him would join in and agree with him.

Ray adored his dad. During one of these rare visits to my house, I overheard him say how much he loved his dad. He said, 'My dad is the greatest dad ever. One day I will build a statue for my dad.' I was full of admiration to hear Ray make a profound statement about his dad. Many fathers are great, but not many sons came up with words of love and respect as Ray did. It was this statement which my God burnt into my heart and used it to place me on Ray's path. Ray became influenced by opinions, which would have led him to unwelcomed existence, and it would have broken his dad's heart. It was this statement I confronted Ray with. It was on 4 December when I was a first-year university student; I spotted Ray going to the canteen to meet his fellow students. I waited outside, watching the only entrance to the canteen.

As he came out, I walked towards him and mumbled with a shaky voice, 'Could I speak to you please for a minute?' He

49

smiled, totally gobsmacked by my request. He knew how shy I was. This was a huge step for me to take. The next minute, I spoke with a boldness, which surprised both of us. I said to him, 'Is this the statue, which one day I heard you saying, you were going to build for your father?' We were both shocked, to say the least, of what came out of my mouth. We paused for a minute. He knew exactly what I was referring to. For once, Ray was lost at words. He was told off, but he was intrigued. We avoided any eye contact. He pretended to be pushing a little stone with his foot.

He then hit back and said, 'Why does it matter to you?'

I replied, 'It would be a shame to lose the special relationship you have with your dad.' We very briefly glanced at each other, and that was the end of the encounter. Since, every time Ray came to visit my brother, he would say hello to me. He noticed me, and a spark had started. Much later, we were in love.

We could not enjoy love when the whole country was cursed with war. Iran-Iraq war was dictating life. A life that was miserable for everybody. War songs were all we hear on the radio and on television. War songs were even sung during wedding celebrations as if they were woven into our minds. Their words, horrible and as graphic as they were, singing them on a daily basis was the norm. Nobody knew what tomorrow would bring. Many hundreds of thousands of young men lost their lives in a pointless war. Two countries hated by the rest of the world yet the richest in oil production battling over what? Why did the war start? Why did it continue? Only a few people knew. The few whose minds were controlled by evil. Those who had no regard for human life or the miserable existence of millions of innocent citizens. You cannot be human and have anything to do with rivers of blood, total brokenness, and the destruction of a whole country. Till the present day, millions of people are still suffering, both living inside or outside Iraq. The power of darkness had descended and stayed over Iraq for forty long years.

Just as God used me to correct her son's wrong path, Miriam, in turn, made a similar statement one day, which changed my path for the rest of my life. Although I do not know what conversation she had with her husband, Miriam made it clear she wanted me as a daughter in law, and no other girl would do. Ray's dad would have preferred a rich girl from a classier family, but of course, he ended up with me. Despite his dad's effort to persuade him to look elsewhere, Ray was firm yet polite with his dad as he insisted on his choice. With both Ray and his mum on my side, Ray's dad agreed. So, we were engaged.

My family house meant the world to me. It was the last house where I felt I belonged. Within its walls and on my last day as one of its occupants, I got ready as a bride. On my wedding day, Ray's family and his relatives drove to my parents' house. There were people everywhere, inside and outside the house, noise, colour songs, and tears too. The wedding was a ceremony not very well rehearsed but followed by all. Following the customs of the day, I was given lots of gold jewellery to wear, the gift of choice for the bride. The unexpected spoiler of the day was the fringe I was given by the hairdresser without even consulting me. I don't suit fringe. I never had one, yet this total stranger woman decided she was giving me one and on my wedding day. Happy noises filled the air with lots of singing, dancing and the playing of traditional musical instruments. Two new words for you, my reader, 'D'hole' and 'Zoorna', the two Musial instruments played at weddings. Everybody would drive to the church first to attend the wedding service. The party would then head to the wedding reception. Weddings always attracted crowds. As the cars drove from one destination to another, the drivers on the roads, wedding guests, or otherwise would beep the horn constantly. The whole neighbourhood would know when there was a wedding taking place, noisy of course, but a happy one.

Abiding by the tradition of that period, when a young lady got married, she would belong to her husband. Her in-laws became her new family. Therefore, the wedding was usually a sad occasion for the brides' family. They would always have mixed feelings: a happy one to see their daughter getting married and hopefully to a decent man but a sad one too. She will not be part of this family anymore, a visitor perhaps, occasionally. So, when it was my turn to be a bride, and as I was exiting my parents' house, it pained me knowing what I was leaving behind. Burning tears spoiled my makeup, and my words stayed buried inside me. Although my siblings and my mother felt my pain, and they too had watery eyes, but seeing my father wiping his tears crushed my heart. That was the first time ever I saw my father crying. Yet, he must have thought I would be living five miles away. None of us anticipated what the future outlook was. My parents' presence in my life and their memories stopped there. A year after my wedding, I made another journey. This time to leave the country altogether to join my husband in Oxford.

Despite all the sadness for transitioning from one household to the next, from one family to another, and from one existence to a totally different one, yet it was my wedding day. Ray had to travel to Oxford at the end of September, so the wedding had to take place in a few weeks' time. It was a miracle to organise a wedding in an existence in which sanctions dictated what was available and what was not. In those days' invitation cards were dropped off by hand. You could never tell how many more extra guests would accompany those you had invited. The food was cooked in the house as there were no catering facilities in those days. Any spare hands willing to help were grabbed with gratitude – relatives, friends and neighbours. The two weeks before the wedding were a summer of love and busyness. My wedding cake was fourteen layers plus two extra spare ones in case they ran out of cake. The band sang wedding and love songs; no war songs were allowed that night. Both Ray and his father had white suits on. It was such a joyous occasion. Food and drink were in abundance, so were flowers, happy sounds and happy faces everywhere. Over five hundred guests attended our wedding. You had to invite everybody and everybody's friends and neighbours. The adults would be accompanied by an army of children.

Ray had eighteen days after the wedding before he had to fly back to Oxford. I, however, lived with his parents and his four brothers until the following summer. I became the middle child of a new family. I moved to my new house with one piece of advice only from my mother. 'Work hard, my daughter. Make sure you help your mother-in-law. Soft ground will always absorb much water.' I knew what she meant. I promised her I wouldn't let her down.

Chapter 6

A Wedding Gift

A few weeks before the wedding, I had asked Ray, 'Where will I get money from, if and when I need it while you are away?'

He replied, 'Ask my dad as he will be your dad too.' We both knew with my timid nature; I would never ask his dad for money. We did not speak of the subject again. I would never ask my parents either as I should be the one giving them money, not asking for it. Although I was living the dream, yet I was facing the unknown. Everything changed. I would be living with Ray's family while he was away, total strangers to me. My surroundings were new, my room was new and unfamiliar, a new house and neighbourhood. Even the washbasin and the mirror above it were different, yet I kept looking at the mirror to confirm I was still me. I had to win over his dad, who did not want me there to start with. Then there were their relatives and family friends. Deep in my heart, I believed in He who had brought me thus far would find a way.

When I asked Ray what would I do for money when he was away, the Heavens heard my need too, and unlike Ray's answer, I received THE answer. My God heard me, and He was quick to answer. Ibn Al Bitar was an Irish hospital in Baghdad. It was a dream place to work in. The doctors and the surgeons, as well as all the healthcare staff, the management and the admin were either Irish or British. Due to the sanctions imposed on the country, and the travel restrictions imposed by the government, ordinary people could not travel abroad. Men between the age of eighteen and forty-five were recruited in the army fighting at the front. They were not allowed to leave the country. Men older than forty-five years old were recruited as the Army of the People. Travel restrictions were applied to them too. Women were not allowed to travel on their own unless accompanied by an adult male relative. Where could they find a male relative to accompany them? Ibn Al Bitar hospital was created to treat patients in the country instead of sending them abroad. A friend of mine used to work there. She had suggested I fill in an application form to work as an interpreter. I did, and for months I heard nothing. To my surprise, I was asked to go for an interview only days before my wedding. At the end of the interview, I was asked, 'Can you start work on Monday?'

Totally unexpected, yet filled with excitement and warm feeling, I replied: 'I cannot come on Monday as it is my wedding day.' So it was agreed I would start the following Monday. No words could describe my gratitude.

Throughout my life, I had my faith to sustain me, but never before it was felt so real, so here, so now. My God did not just give me any job; this job was like a powerful flood of goodness which He showered me with. Many privileges came with the job I did not even know they existed. A wedding gift from my Father above. I had a salary before I entered Ray's house. My salary was more than both my in-laws' salaries put together. I had a driver to take me to work and back. My meals were free. My uniform was free. Making phone calls abroad and posting mail to the outside world was almost impossible, not for me. I could phone Oxford in the evenings and speak with Ray in privacy directly from the hospital's switchboard. Ms Hays, the sister in charge, let me use her mail address at the hospital to receive my letters from Ray. My four brothers-in-law in-law enjoyed my access to the hospital library of movie videos, free of charge. Movies they could not get hold of anywhere in the country. Every week, I would borrow three movies for them to enjoy. Their favourites were horror as the state-run two TV channels would not show this kind of genre. By the time I stopped working at the hospital, my brothers would have had watched all the available movies. As trade with the outside world was totally controlled by the government, chocolate was a commodity. You could not get it anywhere. We did not know all the varieties, how it looked like, and never knew how it tasted like. You could imagine how pleased my four brothers were when I would come back from the hospital with big carrier bags filled with all sorts of chocolate. The staff who I worked with would bring them back after visiting Britain or Ireland on their vacation. My brothers liked having me around as they were allocated house chores prior to my arrival, but the day I entered their house, their chores became my chores, cleaning the house, helping with preparing meals, and many dinner parties, which they hosted. I was grateful for the way my brothers accepted me, as it must have been such an upheaval for them to have a girl in the house. They treated me well. Being the head of the family, I gave my salaries to my father-in-law; he objected, but I insisted.

Being married to the person I loved, knowing I would be joining him at Oxford the following year, and having a great job, life could not have been any better, considering what the country was going through. Yet, my heart had its unfulfilled wishes related to the life I had before my marriage. Working as an interpreter at Ibn Al Bitar Hospital, I was the source of much money, yet in my inability to pass some of my income to my mother was a sore point in my heart. When I was a young girl, I made a promise to myself to spend my first salary on my mother. It never happened.

My brother, who was three years older than me, a qualified engineer, was working as a landmine disposal engineer in the army. He earned peanuts as his monthly salary, the cost of half a dozen eggs. Despite how dangerous my brother's work was, we were still grateful as it meant he was not fighting the enemy face to face, the fate of many of his friends. My brother was single, and his yet to happen wedding would have been a big burden for my mum. A small fortune was needed to have him married. As it was the tradition in those days, marriage was part of life when you are at a certain age, wartime or peacetime. This agonising fact would have been on my mother's mind all the time. And it was on my God's mind too. He showed up, again, when I needed Him most. My God and I have a great relationship. He had used people around me, situations, even a little sparrow to speak to me and make His presence real.

I was based at the Physiotherapy department at Ibn Al Bitar. This was the least significant department in the hospital. Other interpreters did not regard it as important as the wards in which they were based in. Not many patients needed Physio as part of their care plan. However, one day, a patient arrived accompanied by many security guards. I had no idea who he was since all men wore army uniforms. To think of it now, men wore army uniforms everywhere, including when visiting relatives, basically whenever they did not have their pyjamas on. The patient was none but the minister of petroleum! He was referred to the physio department to be shown various exercises related to his condition. In those days, people like him ruled the world. They had so much power and influence. He was probably third in command in the country. I believe, without a shadow of a doubt my God used this man to reach out to me. God poured out His blessings with great power you could not help but stop and wonder, then shut up and worship.

I was a painfully shy person, only spoke when spoken to and only to answer a question. I never started a conversation. So naïve and innocent with the mind of a child. The Minister of Petroleum said to me, 'Your English is good. Where did you learn it?'

I replied, 'I was taught it at school and at university.'

He continued, 'What university you went to, and what did you study?'

I gave him an answer, which unsettled him. 'I am a graduate with a degree in Petroleum Engineering.' He felt very awkward. It did not sit with him well to have a Petroleum Engineer yet working as an interpreter. The unprompted smile on his face and his unpolished choice of words that followed said it all; the system had failed me. Let me say, in an ideal world, with no war and living in a country that is floating on oil; I could be earning hundreds of thousands of pounds, so no wonder he felt uncomfortable.

So, he said, 'What made you do Petroleum Engineering?'

I replied, 'My older brother was at university doing the same course, which got me interested.'

The next question, the most important one, was 'Where does your brother work?' My words, which followed, were like a hook, and he was caught.

I said, 'He is working as a Landmine Engineer with the army.' His next words were coming from above as my God used this man's mouth to deliver His next bundle of blessings for my family and me.

Minister exclaimed, 'Since we could not help you, and offer you a position to suit your qualification, surely we can help your brother.' His best words followed. 'Ask your brother to come and see me next Saturday.' Saturday was the start of the following week. Feeling good about himself, he continued boasting about the great opportunity he had on offer for my brother. The post was based in the city. My brother would be sent abroad for mandatory training to Ireland and Japan.

I could not wait to get home and phone my mother to give her the great news. I imagined my brother on his wedding day and my mother wearing a beautiful dress for the occasion. This job would transform my family's life. A huge burden would be lifted off my mother's shoulder. There was nothing I could give the Minister as a thank you gift. Days after, I visited my artist friend and picked the biggest and the most glamorous looking piece of art I could buy, suitable for a Minister with a heavenly mission. The next time the special patient came for his next physio appointment, I had the gift waiting for him. Holding the gift with a big smile on his face, he was very impressed. He knew he could not find anything like it in the whole country.

I only worked at Ibn Al Bitar Hospital for one year. Next time I saw Ray was the following summer. So, I gave up my job at the hospital and packed my suitcase. When Ray travelled back to Oxford, this time I was his companion. Unfortunately, I was not at home to attend my brother's wedding, but I heard about it. Apparently, it was a great day. There was enough money to cater for a great gathering. Much more was left over to give my brother a good start in life. My brother's wedding took place during even harsher times due to the Iran-Iraq war. My father-in-law, in my absence, used his influence and his contacts and became a wedding planner again. He was the star of the show. He managed to get a supply of food, drink and even alcohol at times when everything was sold with rations. I heard about the wedding when I was in Oxford. I was very grateful to my father-in-law. I never asked or expected the part he played in my brother's wedding. My father-in-law said to me, 'Since you were in Oxford, and you had to miss your brother's wedding, I took it upon myself and acted on your behalf to support your brother in any way I could.' That was a turning point in my relationship with my father-in-law. He started regarding me as a daughter rather than a daughter in law.

Chapter 7

At Oxford

By the time I finished saying my goodbyes, I was emotionally drained, yet I persuaded myself to focus on the positives. My future was sorted. I married the person I loved. The good times and the good life were about to start. The plan was to join Ray for a year or two if needed and then return home. Nobody knew what the future had in store for us.

Being inside Baghdad airport and, later on, boarding a plane were new experiences to me as I had never been abroad. With every minute passed, my head was bombarded with new information. Ray, though, had enough confidence for both of us. I followed him and copied everything he did. After six hours on the plane, the door was opened, and I found myself at Heathrow airport. It was September. The cold air hit me on the face and gave me the shivers. The first thing which caught my eyes was the sky was not blue! Everything looked different, people looked different, the buildings and the streets were different, the smells were different, and even the air felt heavier to breathe. If I had planned to paste a smile on my face, somehow it did not appear. I must have looked so miserable. I had just left home and everybody I held dear behind. All familiar things were replaced with totally different things. No matter what my eyes captured, it was new. Everything my ears heard was fuzzy. I could not make out what people were saying. It felt like I suddenly became deaf. So, my ears stopped functioning. My eyes were working hard, though. They were like catching two movies running at the same time. I was still watching my home movie of what became my past life, overlapping with every scene around me, which became my present life. Two worlds proved to be extremely different. It had taken me my adult life to adjust.

We had to walk in the streets of London to get to a coach stop. We were going to Oxford. The green colour grabbed my attention. There was so much of it. I kept looking at all the trees around me and the green bushes, expecting to find fruits, but I saw nothing. I kept saying to myself, 'Why would the people here plant trees if the trees do not yield any fruit?' The only comforting thing I saw was blackberry bushes here and there. Every time I passed by one, I smiled first, then my eyes will tear up. The blackberry bushes felt like they were a touch from home, which had followed me. Despite being a short journey, my brain was already oversaturated with new scenes, so it switched off. Even though my eyes were opened, but I stopped seeing. I heard chat, but I recognised no voices, only noise. I so yearned for a cuddle from someone from home, or perhaps by chance, I might see a familiar face as we turn around the next corner. Nothing made sense to me. Even the traffic was going in the opposite direction to what my eyes and brain had got used to, and the drivers were sitting on the wrong side of the vehicle. Although English was my third language, and I had the opportunity to practice it for a whole year while working in Ibn Al Bitar hospital, I thought everybody spoke so fast. Cold faces were rushing around, followed by more cold faces. As everybody around me was walking in a bubble of their own, so I kept walking silently.

We got on the coach to Oxford. Throughout the journey, I was staring at the scenery outside, too tired to even speak. In less than an hour, we arrived at Oxford. Ray and I were walking towards what became my next home. We were dropped off at the top of the road where the house was. I was all emotions, hot and raw. My heart was pounding with excitement mixed with loss. The ground under my feet felt so shaky and sticky as if I did not have any control over my steps. It felt like when you sit on your ankle for a long time. My head and my legs were wobbly. With every step I took, the home was becoming a distant light in the darkness which engulfed me, like a dot in the horizon behind me. Once I got at the front door, the door to home I had left behind was shut. Little I knew then; it did shut, and forever. My new dwelling looked so small, stuffy and no sunlight. The minute Ray opened the front door, I was faced with narrow stairs. A very small hall area on my left led to the kitchen. The first door on my left was shut. Ray walked past it to the second door on the left and opened it. We dropped the suitcases on the floor. The room was so small. The ceiling was so low it felt like I could touch it if I stood on my toes. Soon enough, it was obvious that we did not have the whole house for ourselves; we only had this one room. I stood next to my suitcase, not sure what to do next, not wanting to sit down, and knowing going back home was not an option. I felt like a child, but I had to act like an adult. Those negative thoughts were not shared with Ray, the numbing feelings as if my internal organs were combusting. I forced myself to take deep breaths and embrace the new chapter of my life. A new door opened, and out of a time machine, I came out.

Ray had rented out one bedroom in shared accommodation in Gipsy Lane. Our room was the largest but had no window. Bryan, the landlord, had extended the room and added a double French door, which opened to the driveway in the back of the house. I looked at Ray; he had a beautiful smile on his face. He said, 'Let me show you around.' With a charming and beautiful smile like that, I smiled back and followed him as a queen accompanying her king, introducing her to his kingdom and to his subjects. We shared the bathroom and the kitchen with four total strangers: a middle-aged driving instructor, a solicitor, a fellow student and Tina. Another temporary existence, and in no time, we would be going back home with two postgraduate degrees from England.

Ray was too busy to spend any time with me. He would leave first thing in the morning, and he wasn't back till seven in the evening. He was in the middle of preparing for his PhD degree. He was excused for working long hours. I enrolled at Oxford Brooks University, the former Oxford Polytechnic, to study various modules in Maths and Computing. Adjusting to the new lonely way of life took its toll on me. I missed home, and it upset me not attending church. Christmas day came and went, and we did not celebrate Christmas as we used to do at home. I had never before missed Christmas service. Days after, I was walking in the neighbourhood looking for a church. I came across a church building, but it was closed. During this outing, I found out the streets do not have numbers; instead, they each have a unique name. Another huge change to adjust to. At home, the only streets with names would be the big old ones, mainly in the city centre. In residential areas, the neighbourhood would be divided into many areas. Each area had a number. Each area had its streets numbered uniquely, and the houses in each street had either an even or odd number depending on which side of the street the house was. The numbering system made it so much easier to know where you were and how far away from where you want to be you were. And if it happened and you got lost, you could easily navigate your way back home. Not in Oxford, the streets had names, some I could not even read. I decided I was not going to walk too far. Mentally, I kept a note of certain landmarks to help me get back home safely. On Saturdays, Ray and I would walk to a small supermarket, called Budgen, in the Headington area. We would study all week and visit Budgen on Saturdays; welcome to our new life. I loved it. It was our first time living together. Every day, I discovered a new thing about Ray or a new habit of his.

One day, one of the female lodgers, Tina, said to me, 'Would you like to come with me to town?'

I said to myself, 'I hope she will not take me to Budgen.' But I said to her, 'That would be really nice.' We got ready, and off we went. Tina was all smiles and giggles. She was probably a year or two younger than me. With Tina, I discovered the real Oxford, the city of dreaming spires. Up until the day before, and judging by what I had seen so far, including Budgen, I used to say to myself, 'What is the fuss about Oxford?' Tina helped me to see the magic of Oxford. The bus to town went in the opposite direction to Headington. In less than ten minutes, there it was in all its glory, Oxford. I was in for a treat. Everything I saw was breath-taking, and its buildings were out of this world. There are no less than 38 colleges in Oxford. We went through Cornmarket, the main shopping street. We went inside St Michael church, which is the oldest building in Oxford. Tina pointed out the oldest pub in the city as we passed by it. We walked along the High Street and over Magdalen Bridge. You could lose yourself for hours facing The Radcliffe Camera in Radcliffe Square, admiring its history and beauty. We passed by the Ashmolean Museum on Beaumont Street, which is Britain's oldest public museum. It claims to be the world's oldest museum. The magnificent buildings of various colleges are so rich in history. We visited so many shops. I remember buying a little bottle of White Musk from one of the little shops in a narrow alley. White Musk continued to be my favourite smell for the time I stayed in Oxford. Many people would cycle as the roads were so narrow and busy with people everywhere. In the month of July, it was better to avoid going to the city centre as it was filled with young European students visiting, probably to attend summer language schools.

After a few months at Oxford, I had the pleasure of standing at the top of Gipsy Lane, waiting impatiently for the coach coming from London. I had a special visitor on the coach. It was my brother, no less. He was on his way to Ireland for a business trip. As part of his training course, he was going to spend several months in Ireland. I was over the moon to see him. I saw all my family in him. I cooked a meal for my brother; I hadn't done this before, of course. We had a great night. We stayed up till the early hours. My brother's visit filled my heart with joy unspeakable. It was a confirmation and the fulfilment of God's provision. So, my brother now had an amazing job, working not as an Engineer in the Army defusing deadly mines which could've exploded in his hand at any moment and killed him, oh no, he was working as a Petroleum Engineer. He was earning lots of money. Indeed, this visit was the making of his financial riches. After Ireland, it was Japan he travelled to. Another training course and another opportunity to accumulate even more money than the visit to Ireland. He had more money than what my mother would've needed to see him married and settled. God is great. This was one of many occasions which even winning the lottery would have never compared. The petroleum minister had met my brother, and a new chapter in my brother's life had started. With a heart filled with gratitude, I looked up to heaven, gave thanks, and said, 'Who am I Lord to deserve this?' In my eyes, I was a filthy old rag, and in my father's eyes, I seemed to be worth it! My brother stayed one night, and the next morning he was on his way to Ireland. My brother's visit was like a little bird coming from heaven above to let me know my God keeps His promises, so be at peace.

Chapter 8
Israel

Ray was keen for me to study a postgraduate course. There were so many universities to choose from with so many different master's degrees on offer. We discussed our options and contemplated what could be an ideal one for employment for when we return home. We picked a master's degree in Software Engineering. It was a conversion course which ran for one year. The course was not offered in Oxford, so we had to find a closer university that offered this course. This was the late eighties, and computing was just starting to become noticed as a profession. I applied to various universities, and I got an offer from Birmingham University. Although I was miserable in Oxford, at least, I had Ray's company in the evenings. In Birmingham, I had to be on my own all the time. No wonder I was dreading the move. I lived in university halls which were near Edgbaston. Male students lived in the ground floor flats, and the female students lived on the floor above. I shared the flat with five other girls; each one had enrolled in a different postgraduate course. Only one of the flatmates was a local girl; the rest were exploring Birmingham for the first time as I did. There were girls from Ghana, South Korea, London, and China with me. How did we survive with one bathroom and a small kitchen? I have no idea. The Chinese girl would cook her lunch and dinner every day in the flat, all with fresh ingredients. She would take her time as if she was the only person who needed to use the kitchen and the cooker. Then the South Korean girl would bring her boyfriend, and together they would occupy the bathroom for as long as they saw fit with no care in the world. It surprised me how they had no regard for other occupants. Obviously, I could not complain since Ray would come and visit me at least once a month, so he too would stay in my room and therefore use the facilities in the flat. Ray made new friends with other postgraduate students who he recognised from home. Ray's new friends lived in nearby halls. It was five minutes' walk from mine. Ray would go and spend some time with these guys and enjoy the opportunity to add another dimension to his life.

At home, since my first day at primary school, I was taught Israel was our enemy. This was the case in the neighbouring countries in the Middle East too. We were being indoctrinated to accept Israel as our enemy and the forbidden association. This was one of many situations that once we were inside our family home, the outside world's rules and doctrines were left outside. Being Christian, we were a minority. It was not easy. We knew we were different. You had to develop quick wisdom to distinguish between our beliefs and what you were taught at school. Although we did not agree with the opinions of the world around us, we still could not publicly shout it out loud. Probably what made it, at times, even harder was having my father's first name as Moshe. It was an awful situation to have lived through, especially during the period when an Israeli politician and defence minister in those days was called Moshe Dayan. At school, we lived with discrimination at the hand of some teachers. As a family, we persevered, and my dad kept his name as Moshe. Many a time, it was hinted to us, suggested, even told at times to change my father's first name. Many Christian families with Old Testament biblical names ended up changing them to more secular ones. My relative ended up changing his name Israel to Ismael.

When television was still broadcasting in black and white in the late seventies, there was a drama series called *The Fugitive*. The main character was played by the actor Richard Campbell. Everybody loved watching this program. We could not wait for the next episode to be broadcasted the following week. It was by far my big brother's favourite drama of all time. Probably towards two-third through the series, someone in the authorities came to know either the producer or the director or someone involved in the making of this drama was Jewish. That was it. They stopped broadcasting it. We never knew what happened to the fugitive as we never had the chance to see the rest of the episodes. And so, it was in Birmingham, and for the first time, I read the word Israel on an item I held in my hands. I read the country of origin of a fresh herb I bought from the local supermarket. It had the name Israel on it. I don't know what happened to my mind, but I held the herbs in my hand and stood still for a while. I honestly didn't know why my tears were flowing. Were they tears of joy, like when you see someone you had missed for so long? Were they tears of sadness as to say why we had to accept stupid rules made by a few idiots to deny us basic rights? Israel was forbidden, the unknown, and the unspoken truth. The first time I ever heard of the tragedy of the

Holocaust was when I was in Oxford. It never appeared in the history lessons which I was taught or any literature I came across.

I could not eat the herb. Holding it in my hands felt like I was holding all of Israel in my hand. I didn't know what to do with it. I started chatting with my Father above. 'I know what I am thinking of is laughable, but I want to believe it.' So, I prayed with all of my heart. 'Lord Jesus, I know you lived and walked in many streets and places in the Holy Land. Since this herb had grown in the holy land too, maybe, just maybe, there is a chance of one in a trillion that the soil in which this herb was planted in had a tiny particle which had touched your feet.' I paused. I repeated this statement to myself this time, and suddenly it was: *could this really happen? Wow! Who can say no to this?* I could be holding a plant that might have touched a particle of soil or tiny gravel that could have touched Lord Jesus' feet. I got so overwhelmed. It was like I was in His presence. I felt heat shining from every cell in my body. My tiny room felt like a never-ending expanded space. I was floating in another dimension. If only I could've released my spirit, it would've soared to infinity. My ears were hot and blocked to the outside world. My physical body couldn't comprehend what I was experiencing. I sat on the floor, and I closed my eyes and worshiped.

I hung the bunch of herbs on the wall where my desk was. I would gaze at it while I was studying in my little room. The bunch of herbs was the first thing I looked at when I entered my room and the last thing before I left. I would kiss it many times a day. When the herb became very dry, I would bring my hand so close to it, pretending I touched it. I would then kiss my hand. It was like my physical link to my Saviour. It filled me with joy and peace.

I did struggle both academically and emotionally. There were not enough hours for me to learn all the thirteen new subjects and do the course work. As computing students in the late eighties, we didn't have the resources which are available today. However, we were given twenty-four-hour access to one of the computing labs. Many times, I had to spend the whole night in the lab. I would enter the lab after the last lecture and only leave at 9:00 am the following morning. The computers were so primitive. If you wanted to compile and run your program, you had to delete all files and only keep the source code. One Saturday, after spending the night before in the lab, I caught a bus at the campus, which took me to the city centre to buy a few necessities. I climbed to the top decker of the bus and rested on the seat, totally shattered and desperate for a wee nap. Two teenage boys were sitting behind me, chatting away. One of them said so casually, 'I have three hours to kill.' Three hours to kill! How I wished they could've lent me these three precious hours.

There was a narrow path in the far end where the halls were situated. Sometimes, I would use the path as a shortcut to walk to university buildings. There were trees and short thick bushes on one side. The other side was the bottom of a steep hill, which was covered with grass and wildflowers. The end of the path took me to behind Apple's building and then to the main road. The sight of the hill awakened in me the desire to climb up to the top and roll down as I used to do when I was a child. My little friends and I would race to the top of any hill we saw and roll down many times on end. And when there were no hills in sight, we would just do it on any grassy area. I promised myself I would let loose and do it one day when nobody was around as I was aware of other students passing through that path. I had to wait for the right moment. One day, that moment arrived. I was feeling down, homesick, and just overwhelmed with the excessive demand for the course and life in general. I was so sad I didn't even know what to pray for. I had no option but to complete the course. I was exhausted and almost lost my fighting spirit. My brain was stretched to the limit. I was so miserable. I thought it was time to let go for a while and act stupidly. I didn't care if there were other people around or not. I climbed to the top of the hill, lied down on the grass, folded my arms on my chest, and rolled all the way down. I underestimated how steep the hill was. My body was rolling down much faster than I had thought and not listening to my brain's instructions to slow down. Being older, you would be heavier, so gravity played its part and made the experience a little bit scarier. I was not enjoying the thrill of it at all. After a few seconds, I got really scared. I couldn't stop myself. I didn't know where my rolling body was heading. I was lucky there weren't any rocks on my way. Finally, I did reach the bottom. My body halted with a jerk. My head was spinning, and I was feeling sick. I had to sit on the grass for a wee while waiting to be sick, but I was spared the experience. I kept my head bent down for a while, and I took many deep breaths. My clothes and I were a mess. I was covered with mud and grass all over me. Still, I felt so much better for getting it out of my system. It felt like I had a telling off, smacked by the wild grass and told to snap out of feeling sorry for myself. I went back to my room sheepishly, thinking nobody saw me or heard me.

I was wrong. I needed help, and my God showed up again. He put in my path a British Indian girl called Pari. She was enrolled in my course, but she had completed her BSc Hons in Computing and Maths at Birmingham University the year before. Pari was privately educated. Her parents lived in an area, which was deemed to be far enough for Pari to be granted university accommodation. She stayed in a different hall of residence to mine, but it was within walking distance. Pari was to me like an angel in the body of a person. I had asked for permission from my lecturers to place my tape recorder at the front of the lecture theatre. I would tape each lecture, listen to the recording in the evenings, and make my own notes. Pari approached me one day. She introduced herself and then she asked me about the tape recorder. She asked if I could lend her the tapes once I had finished with them. The tapes proved to be the start of a lifeline. Pari was enrolled in some of the subjects I was studying. As for the rest, she had already achieved them during her BSc course. Pari had kept all her notes from earlier years. The next day when she came to my room, she brought with her every piece of paper she had kept for the subjects I needed, including lecture notes, textbooks, and exercises with answers. She knew the place, the university buildings, the lecturers, the system, and even the janitors, unlike me. With her little green mini car, she drove me around the city to do our weekly shopping, to her parents' house, and even to end of the year show of her Indian singing and dancing school. I couldn't have picked a better companion for me. My Father in heaven knew my needs, and each and every one was fulfilled in the person of Pari. With time, life in Birmingham became a bit bearable, but I couldn't wait to go back to Oxford.

I had to pass closed book written exams for thirteen subjects, the ongoing programming assignments, and a final closed book programming exam. I am convinced I could have never achieved this on my own. I know my God had to put together another miracle plan to get me through living in Birmingham, and Pari was the plan. When life was difficult and mean, then when goodness came my way, I would look up and give thanks. I finished my summer project, got my master's degree, and with my little one inside my tummy, I moved back to Oxford.

Chapter 9

Daffodils

When I returned to Oxford, Ray had secured another accommodation for us. We moved to Banbury Road on the north side of the city. Houses on Banbury Road were huge, and therefore I guess some of them weren't used as family homes but for other purposes. Ray and I rented out a room in a place that was owned and run by the local church. The trustees of the building wanted to create a nice warm dwelling place for overseas students. This accommodation was meant to be a place with a difference, run like a business, but influenced by Christian values.

Living on Banbury Road gave us the opportunity to get to know Mr and Mrs Bennett, a lovely couple who ran the place. Their accommodation was on the first floor of the building. To add to many job titles they attained, Mr and Mrs Bennett were missionaries at earlier years in their lives. A lovely couple whose friendship we treasured and kept till the present time. As I was expecting my first child, Mr Bennett gave us a much bigger room to live in. It was classified as a family room. It was more like a studio flat. We had a living area, the kitchenette and the bed, all in one space. There was a door that opened to a closet in which you could hardly fit a single bed.

I also squeezed the baby cot at the end of the single bed along the way. It was so tiny you couldn't even shut the door. We shared the bathroom with other residents. Ray was at the final stage of writing up his PhD theses. Apart from textbooks, we didn't have many earthly possessions. The place was big enough for the soon to be three of us. A year later, we were joined by Ray's dad. And after that, his brother followed. The place ended up being the home of the five of us, tight of course, but enriched with endless fond memories and tales to tell.

But before that, when it was just Ray and me yet, being three months pregnant, my little bump started showing. Morning sickness continued throughout my pregnancy; in fact, I was sick even in the morning Sarah was born. I started looking for a job, any job to help with our living expenses. I went to an employment agency which was based in the city centre. Soon I was offered a job at the City Council's Housing department. It was a part-time job, and I was paid weekly. Every Friday, the agent will phone the head of the department to find out if my services were still required. To my delight, the answer was yes, and it continued to be for the following months. I was touched by the courtesy shown to me as I was always asked first if it was OK for me to continue working for another week. My tummy was getting big, but I was delighted to have been kept on. In fact, I continued working until two weeks before Sarah was born. However, towards the latter stages of my pregnancy, I had to get a letter from my GP to confirm I was fit enough for work. The wages I received covered our weekly shopping. Every morning Ray would take the bus to Headington, and I would head to the City Centre. Once I had finished my hours at work, I would go to Ray's office and wait till he finished work. We would catch the bus back home together at the end of the day. While waiting for Ray to finish for the day, I taught myself to touch-type on the computer using free software. Soon enough, my typing speed was good enough. I started typing Ray's thesis rather than paying for a professional typist. This was the late eighties, and the mainframe computers ruled the business world; PCs were not born yet. Every day, Ray would handwrite what his brain produced for the day, and I would be waiting impatiently to get typing. There were days when Ray would be occupied with other duties, so I was made redundant. A day would merit being productive if Ray had written at least six pages. As every pregnant woman would tell you, the last few weeks are always the hardest. Ray would tell you the same about writing a PhD thesis. We were both fed up towards the end. I was pregnant with my baby, and he was pregnant with his PhD thesis.

Ray and I were content with our lives, yet our families still continued to survive through the Iran-Iraq war. The sanctions continued to limit what they could have access to. Ray's brothers would contact us to let us know the kind of items they needed to ship home, including equipment for their photography studio. War or not, people needed their photos taken, mainly passport sized ones. In those days, there were no photo booths in supermarkets providing you with instant photos. The business was good, and any extra income generated was appreciated.

I started looking for a church. Sunday was the Lord's Day. If I wasn't in the house of God on Sundays, I didn't feel right. I would be in a bad mood. I went out for walks in the neighbourhood searching for one. I found a church. It was a big milestone in my life. I found St Andrews church. The church was off Banbury Road. It was probably ten minutes' walk from where we lived. I loved the church, and I loved belonging to it. The church injected into my life unspeakable joy. This was the first time I heard children talk during church service. It dawned on me how giving the children their place, their importance, and their portion of the worship was remarkable. I didn't know St Andrews was an Anglican church. I thought all churches were Catholic. I wasn't aware of having other variations of the Christian faith. Although I did notice a few differences in the order of the service and the way it was conducted, however, it didn't register with me. I said to myself, 'This is the English way of worship, I guess.' I loved the preaching, listening to the word of God explained to me. I was like a sponge. I couldn't get enough. I started reading the Bible to myself at home rather than being read to me in the church. I now had a Bible. While living in students' halls at Birmingham the year before, I found a hardback Bible in my room. A light brown coloured thick book. It was inside the top drawer of my bedside table. I thought it was for me. I didn't know who to ask, but when I left Birmingham, I took the Bible with me. This was my first ever Bible. Did I steal it? Was I meant to leave it there and only read it while I stayed in that room? I don't know. I took it and kept it all these years. I get warm feelings every time I open my light brown NIV Bible, even though I've owned so many other ones since. Going to church added a whole new experience to my existence. The church service was conducted differently from how it used to be done at home, where the priest will recite his part and the deacon will recite his, and somewhere in between, a song or two will be sung, which gave the congregation a chance to participate. Nowadays, at home, the church service is more alive despite the size of the congregation being shrunk to a tenth of what it used to be. I was brought up as a Catholic, but soon, I felt I need to be identified as a Christian rather than a Catholic. I was not giving up on Catholicism or anything. I came up with my own version of being a Christian. God was the centre of my life, and that is what mattered to me most. As for domination, I see it as a label given by humans, not by my God. I was proud of being a follower of Christ. Although I don't like the word proud, but I have to state boldly being a follower of Christ is the only thing in my life I am very proud of.

Having my first baby, my Sarah, made me aware of how alone I was. As clever and talented Ray was in his field, he didn't have a clue about most of life's matters. And when it came to babies, he had nothing to offer. Many years later, and as my three babies became three beautiful young ladies, Ray suddenly became the one with lots to offer. He is the one the three of them would turn to. They would prefer to discuss any subjects with their dad and seek his approval of whatever they had on mind. And if it happened, Ray and I were disagreeing on a topic, the three of them would for sure take his side no matter what – how roles have turned around. Their dad is like no other, and they would choose him before me any minute and every time. Mind you, I would too. He was very patient, sincere, and solid. What a father should be.

Sarah's birth was on a Friday. Ray was back from university, tired and hungry. It was around 7:00 pm, and dinner was on the table. And suddenly, while I was just about to eat my dinner, my water broke. It was one of those moments where you freeze with eyes and mouth wide open;

you stop breathing, waiting to hear an instruction as to what to do next, and the instruction doesn't arrive. I didn't know what to do. I stopped eating, of course, cleaned the mess, and kept myself busy as I didn't know what will happen the next minute or the next hour. The pain started. It was like no other pain. I felt physically unable to hide my weakness any longer in case I hurt Ray's feelings. It was then when I started calling my mother with tears rolling down my face. I needed her so desperately. In fact, any one of my sisters would've done. My hospital bag was ready. I took everything out and put it back in again without thinking. I washed the dishes quickly, sorted any mess in the room, and had a quick shower. I felt sorry for Ray since if I didn't know what to do, I wonder what was going on in his mind. I would be away for a few days; this means he would need to do everything for himself and find out how to get to the hospital. I fetched the booklet I was given by the health visitor and scanned the content very quickly, looking for the bit which told me what to do when you are in labour. I phoned the number I was given. I was instructed to wait until the interval between the contractions was twenty minutes.

There was a party going on downstairs as it was Mr and Mrs Bennett's retirement party. There were probably more than fifty guests enjoying themselves and celebrating the work and life journey of the esteemed couple. Being a committed Christian and an upright citizen, Sarah's birth made Mr Bennett ignore these facts, and instead, he ended up acting recklessly. Mrs Bennett collaborated too. She said, 'Dear, the baby is coming out, the parents don't have a car, get ready quickly to drive them to hospital.' So, Mrs Bennett tasked Mr Bennett to drive Ray and me to John Radcliff

Hospital. Having enjoyed his retirement party so far, Mr Bennett was drinking alcohol, and he was way over the limit. We arrived at the hospital. I was grateful for having Mr Bennett with us. I got out of the car with much effort. I couldn't walk. It was such a scene to see two hopeless men, childlike action, trying to find a wheelchair for me. The first one they got, they couldn't agree as to how to push it. Soon we figured out the wheelchair didn't work as no matter what and how they steered the stupid thing, it didn't move in the direction it was supposed to go. They soon got a second one, and I was rushed to where I should be. We made it inside safely, and Mr Bennett made it safely back to his party.

Sarah was due on the following Monday, but she had decided she wanted to out on Friday. I gave birth to Sarah at 12:20 am, to be precise. I was in labour for over five hours, but she was worth it. The minute I laid my eyes on her and cuddled her, the pain had already disappeared. You get overwhelmed when you watch this in a movie, or you hold a baby, but the feeling you get when you hold your own baby, this surprise precious gift, no words could describe it. You are too scared even to breathe out while looking down at this living doll.

After Sarah was born, I kept bleeding, and they didn't know what was causing it. Although I was in the hospital, I was attached to a unit run by my GP. I have to say this wasn't a good experience for me at all. My GP was on holiday, and I was left for a while as other doctors won't come to check on me. It was my GP's responsibility. I was about to get a blood transfusion when a replacement doctor arrived. I was given an injection to stop the bleeding. I was sorted. I suppose I was lucky to have survived as God knows how many mothers in the past had lost their lives after childbirth. If only they were given vitamin k injection. This palaver was followed by the most delicious toast and jam in the world. Nothing ever tasted as delicious as that toast and jam. Did the midwives have a magic potion to add to their toast and jam? Perhaps it was having a bite to eat after the sheer exhaustion of giving birth and not having anything to eat for so long.

I left the hospital after five days. During my stay, I was shown how to change the baby, clean her, feed her and bathe her. Basically, everything a new mum needed to know in order to care for her new-born baby. While at the hospital, the midwife made every task seem so easy. Whatever I heard, to my mind, they were words for now. I would nod. Once at home, I had to put everything I was shown to practice, and on my own. Yet this was what qualified me to become a mother.

As we left John Radcliff Hospital, Ray was carrying baby Sarah, not sure if he was doing it right. He was waddling along, and I had to remind him to look where he was going as he kept looking down at Sarah's face. We got inside a taxi, Ray placed my baby in my arms, and the three of us headed home. As the taxi drove through the roads, a journey which was probably twenty minutes long, all I could see on both sides of the roads was a sea of beautiful yellow colour. I didn't even know then what these flowers were, but later on, I learnt they were daffodils. I couldn't take my eyes off my baby's face but only very briefly to see the yellow flowers outside. Since Sarah's birth and until today, every time I lay my eyes on daffodils, I see Sarah's' baby face amongst them. I seek them every year, and it is like I gave birth to them as well as to Sarah. So, every year when we celebrate Sarah's birthday,

I bore the rest of the family as they have to listen to me describing the first time I noticed the sea of daffodils.

Oxford is a stunning city. There was so much history and richness in its architecture. I had the pleasure of living in Oxford for four years. I became a mother in Oxford. This was a good enough reason for me to think of Oxford as a very special place. I met the most amazing people who I learnt so much from. I was lucky enough to get to know a very remarkable lady, Yvonne, and her husband Anthony, Rita and David and many others whose memories I would cherish forever. Yvonne and Anthony lived on the other side of Banbury Road, probably three minutes' walk from where I lived. Yvonne was like my English mother. A very special woman with beauty being the one word to describe her. She was beautiful inside and outside. Sitting next to her and listening to whatever she would say made me feel good. In her company, the outside world did not exist. She would wear bright orange lipstick. She would always have the stick nearby, and from time to time, she would repaint her lips without the need for a mirror. She taught me how to make Sunday roast. Her roast potatoes were the best. So many fond memories. During this time, Ray completed his PhD, a great accomplishment, and an academic dream was fulfilled. My father-in-law had come to visit us in Oxford to attend his son's graduation ceremony. The visit was planned to last a few weeks but ended up being a few years as it never occurred to any one of us what life had in store. In 1990–1991, Iraq went through a second gulf war, and this time it was worse. Iraq invaded the neighbouring country Kuwait. The whole world condemned the ruling regime at home, including Britain. If life was difficult so far, now it became desperate. We had our suitcases packed and ready to go back home. I even had picked gifts for everybody at home. Yet, we found ourselves stranded with world events. We felt like prisoners. Flights to home were cancelled, all communications were cut and so we had to stay put.

I had a toddler, my father-in-law was living with us, our money was frozen, we couldn't go back home and not to mention we were living in Britain, the country which was bombing our families at home. I watched the news, and I would see my homeland lit with fire. The sound of explosions was deafening. I would stand so close to the TV screen every time the news came up, trying to figure out which area had been hit, and could I identify which area it was? More importantly, was it near where our families lived? I would listen to the news, and I would shout out loud, 'No, please no,' begging for it not to be happening. I would shout to the newsreader as if he could hear me. 'Do you know who is living there? Do you know whose sky is this?' Even though the video clip was captured at night-time, the sky looked bloody, lit with fire and explosions. I kept shouting even louder with pain no one could appreciate. 'You are bombing innocent people, my parents, my mother-in-law, our siblings, all our relatives, friends and neighbours, all my life and all my memories are there all the familiar surroundings all the buildings I entered and the streets I walked in.' My home was there, everyone and everything I held dear. It was all getting destroyed, burnt in a colossal way. It looked like hell on earth.

I don't know how I recovered from the mind-numbing out of my control existence. For months, I didn't have any news from home. To add salt to injury, our bank accounts were frozen, and so we didn't have access to any money. There was

Ray, me, Sarah and her grandpa living in a one-room with a kitchenette, sharing the bathroom with God knows how many other people. I must've looked like a zombie to whoever saw me during this period of my life. What do you do?

One day we had a prayer meeting in my little room. The couple leading the meeting was Rita and David. We were studying the scripture which covered the story of Joseph. Rita, being aware of our situation, was trying to comfort us by reminding us how 'God is in control. He plans our lives even though, at times, we don't understand what is going on. Today's big questions will be answered in His time.' She was drawing parallel to our sorrows to those which Joseph went through. We learnt with endurance comes perseverance, strengthened by the hope which we have in the promises of our God. The suffering Joseph had to endure had to happen to allow Joseph to be where he ended up being. It all worked out well as it led Joseph to be in a position to bring about deliverance to his family and turned their tears into joyous celebrations. Joseph was obedient, and he persevered while waiting on God's timing. Rita knew I had questions about why God shut the door on my face, and I couldn't go back home to join my family at home, live with them, or die with them. Rita kept reminding me to trust Him, for He knows, the author of life. Rita would say, 'You are no use to your family if you were at home. God will use you for the salvation of both of your extended families. Just trust Him even when it is hard.' At that moment, I wanted to believe the truths I was hearing, but I didn't know what it all meant. I couldn't see beyond the current moment, so how was my little brain to process it all.

Months later, I received the best news ever; it was in the form of a letter from the Red Cross. All our family members had survived, and no one was hurt. And so, the next chapter of surviving the aftermath of another war started. Sadly, to say though this was not the end yet. In fact, it never was.

My brother-in-law, who is two years younger than my husband, had always dreamt of getting the opportunity to study for a postgraduate degree in England. Ray and I were very cautious with how we spent our cash. We wanted to save enough money to make my brother-in-law's dream come true. Ray was on a mission to find the best suitable course on offer. In God's timing, my brother-in-law was lifted from Iraq and dropped in my little home in Oxford. All I had to do is to open the front door and let him in. What a joy and what a relief? One saved many more to follow.

In the early eighties, you would get three American dollars for one Iraqi dinar. Years later, the Iraqi dinar was not worth the paper which was printed on. For the following ten years, every penny Ray and I made was utilised to help our families to escape the abyss and place them somewhere safer, anywhere in the world. In the meantime, my little family here lived a life of love and care, not much of luxurious worldly goods, but it was a privileged life since God was steering it in the direction which He planned for us.

Balancing it all during this period of my life, I existed as a blind, dumb and deaf person but with feelings that were so raw and a body that was a never healing wound. I was tackling an enormous mission, way beyond my ability. I was like an ant, laden with a load one thousand times its size. The weight of the load on its back almost flattened it. Yet, I had God on my side. I had Him leading. I lived one day at a time with constant silent prayers.

It was sad to accept that my father-in-law's wealth at home became worthless, and somehow Ray and I were the lifelines for our families. God works His miracles if we only trust and obey. One by one, every family member left home and temporarily settled in Jordan, waiting for their immigration papers to get processed and secure the visa for whichever country they ended up immigrating to. Ray and I took care of their living expenses, travel, accommodation, lawyers' fees and paying for private university fee for my youngest brother-in-law to secure his safety and buy time.

I had three part-time jobs. The first one was a childminder for a four-year-old boy called Jamie. I would get Sarah bulked up in her pushchair holding her teddy, and off we were for some fresh air and to get Jamie from school. I would always wait in the same spot near the outdoor cabin, which accommodated Jamie's class so he could see me easily. We would walk back to my room together. If Jamie was tired, I would let him stand on the back of the pushchair holding tightly to the sides in front of me, putting his little feet on the bar on the back of the pushchair. Jamie stayed with me until one of his parents would come and collect him after four o'clock. Jamie loved coming to my little room. He would run and sit on the sofa, glued to my little telly watching the BBC and ITV children cartoon programs. I wasn't sure if his parents would've agreed to a little biscuit or two I gave him, but at times, he would finish off any leftover food from his packed lunch. By the time his parents walked him to his house, all the cartoon programs were over. No wonder Jamie liked being in my room. I don't think I would recognise Jamie if I was to pass him in the streets of Oxford today, but I guess he might recognise me.

My second job was much harder and no fun at all. I was tasked with doing the laundry of the bedding sheets and the covers, washed, dried and ironed for all the rooms of the two buildings of the oversees centre. I am not sure how many they were but to someone like me who hated housework; this was a never-ending job. I didn't mind really since there were two big washing machines and a huge dryer in the building. I used to do the ironing at night when Sarah was asleep. As the space in my room was small, I was keen to get the ironing done and shifted. I was grateful for the financial help we received from the St. Andrews Church as they owned the place. For the period our bank account money was frozen due to the second gulf war, our rent was free. Every week, I used to get a brown envelope pushed under my room door with fifty pounds inside. I never knew who the giver was, but I was moved by the lifeline, which sustained us. Every time I opened the envelope, I saw my God's hand holding the money and placing it in my hand. I don't know if it was one person or a number of St Andrews congregation who contributed, but I was thankful for their generosity. This act of love and care continued till our money was released. At the time, it was Ray, Sarah, Sarah's grandpa, and I who lived in that room, and shortly after, my brother-in-law joined us.

As for the third job, it started as the worst but ended up as the best. It tested me as an individual, but then I was rewarded by divine intervention. My Father above showed up again. This job involved a lovely lady called Maxine. As it happened, there was a little piece of paper on the notice board in the building where I lived, looking for a cleaner for a family of academics with three children. Me and cleaning! If only my mother and my sisters knew, they would've cried first for my state of affairs, but my sisters would've laughed at the same time, saying to themselves, 'Her and cleaning!' So, I phoned to enquire about the job, and I was given the address to go and meet Maxine. Maxine lived in a house less than ten minutes' walk from where I lived. I rang the doorbell and waited for someone to open the door. Maxine flung her front door open and welcomed me like she'd known me all her life. My first observation about Maxine was whether she was talking or not; there was a constant smile on her face. She was a beautiful lady with such warmth and humility; it made me feel good for being alive in a world where people like her existed. We introduced ourselves to each other. She started showing me around, starting with the ground floor, going from one room to another, pointing out what needed to be done and how. We then climbed the stairs to the first floor. She showed me each room explaining whose room it was and a sentence or two about her husband and her three girls. The house had a second floor with more rooms and a bathroom. I had to pay attention to the books, which were scattered all over the place. Some of the books belonged to her daughters, but the rest were borrowed from the local library. The ones with a sticker on the spine of the book belonged to the library. They had to be returned on certain dates, so I was to pile them up and separate them from the rest of the books. With every new info my ears received, I was getting overwhelmed and doubted myself in remembering it all.

Maxine did the talking, and I did the listening. We went downstairs and ended up in the kitchen as she wrapped up the tour of her house. She paused for a minute or two and looked at me, waiting for me to ask a question or to seek some clarification. Throughout the tour, I felt like my inside was a big balloon, and with every word she said, water was getting poured inside me until I was drowning from the inside. Did I have an anxiety or a panic attack, and I failed to diagnose it? I was quiet for an uncomfortable minute or two. She was gazing into my eyes, not sure what to say until I burst into tears. I felt like that ant again. She asked very apologetically what was wrong. Was it something she said? With my face burning and my tears rolling down my face, I said, 'I haven't done any house cleaning job before.' I think at that moment I felt sorry for myself as I hate cleaning and the house was huge for my liking. But I needed the money, so I continued, 'I will do my best to make sure the house will be very clean.' Maxine's heart was probably ten times bigger than any normal heart.

With her eyes welled up, she said, 'I am sure you will.' I did the cleaning in the mornings while my father-in-law looked after Sarah. At the end of the week, my father-in-law and I would walk to a nearby hospital to treat ourselves to a nice cooked lunch in the canteen. We would take turns in pushing Sarah's pushchair. Make no mistake, years later, every time Sarah met her grandpa, he would always remind her how she was the only privileged grandchild who had grandpa pushing her pushchair. He would have never attempted this at home as in those days this was not a man's job.

I gave the cleaning job my best shot. Both Maxine and I were pleased with my cleaning achievement. She would always comment about how she never had her house so clean. Maxine worked from home and travelled to work three times a week. One day as I was finishing cleaning, she was making a cup of coffee for herself. She said to me, 'Would you care to join me?'

Not being rude or anything, I said, 'No, thank you. This is very kind of you.' That didn't stop Maxine from chatting away to me. So, we talked while she was making her cup of coffee, and we talked more while she was drinking it. She asked me about my life. Being an academic, she was keen to find out if I had done any studying. She learnt I had a master's degree in Software Engineering. I told her where I was from and the turmoil which my country was in. She learnt about my father-in-law and his predicament. Maxine listened intently, and every cell in her body was moved.

A few days later, Maxine came to the building where I lived, asking for me. She was holding a bag of tangerines and a cake which she baked for me. Maxine cared, and it made her smile even more beautiful. A few weeks later, she said to me, 'I have been trying to get some research funds, and now I have got it.' She beamed. 'I would like you to work with me as a research assistant; I don't know much about computers. Your computing skills are so much in demand. You will be able to extract information for my research. We could talk about what data I am interested in, ideally, if you could store this data in a database. What do you think?' She didn't wait for my reply. She continued, 'Of course it means instead of cleaning the house, you would be working as a research assistant. You will be an employee of my university, but you will continue to work from my house, so no need to travel to university.' She didn't need to hear my answer as she saw it on my face. I would be working the same hours but with a lot more money, and in an area of my expertise. Walking home that day and repeating Maxine's words had a profound effect on me and changed me from the inside. Even today, when her face comes to mind causes me to get emotional.

Any passer-by who happened to notice me during the ten minutes' walk would've seen a lady with a dreamy look on her face. I knew my God cared for me. So yes, I was over the moon about the new door flung opened for me, but I knew who opened that door, and I knew I mattered to Him. Maxine's research was published. This was followed by a book she wrote using the interesting facts and findings from the database we created together. The work I did for Maxine was on my CV and every job application I filled in during the following years. It was the reason I was offered a better job when we moved to Scotland.

Chapter 10

Janet

We left Oxford as Ray was headhunted and offered a job in Scotland. We rented out a flat in the city which was on floor 17 in a high-rise building. It was a twenty minutes' walk from Ray's work. Sarah was a toddler. My father-in-law came with us and stayed for several months. He then travelled back home as the borders were opened. My brother-in-law started a PhD course in England. Ray's job was too demanding, to say the least. Moving to Scotland meant I had to give up my job with Maxine. I became a housewife for probably nine months until I was offered a job at the university. The flat we had rented was on two floors. Downstairs had the bathroom, a bedroom, and the stairs which led to the top floor, which comprised of the main bedroom, the living room and the kitchen. The three of us shared the bedroom. I couldn't leave Sarah to sleep all alone and abandoned on the lower floor, a whole floor away from me. The living room had a huge window and a door, which led to a small and narrow veranda. Being on floor 17 and having a toddler in the house, this door was locked all the time. We had no furniture, so we ended up spending 120 pounds in a second-hand shop. This money was enough to buy a living room suite, two beds, a fridge freezer, and a washing machine – all second hand but in great condition. We had to make this flat our home. If you have lived on floor 17, then you might have noticed during stormy weather, the light fittings would be moving randomly like crazy. Also, one more observation, I noticed if I leant forward while sitting at the edge of my sofa, I would sense the building moving slightly. Did that scare me? Of course, it did.

My next-door neighbour was a lovely lady called Janet. Janet had a daughter and a son. Her son was married with a family who lived nearby. The son, Matthew, and his family would come and visit Janet from time to time, so I got to meet them. Janet's daughter, Michelle, was probably seven or eight years old. For the first time since my wedding, I was a housewife with lots of free time to fill. Michelle would come and play with Sarah. The two of them spent many hours dressing up dolls and building things. Michelle was a lovely natured girl. She had friends who would come and join her playing with Sarah. Her little friends were Wilson and Richard. They were neighbours too. So, we ended up using the downstairs spare bedroom as the kids' playroom area. Richard lived with his grandpa in the flat across from mine while Wilson lived with his dad on the floor above. Soon, Sarah, Ray and I started going to a local church. The kids wanted to come with us, so I had to ask for permission from their families. Every Sunday morning, the three of them would join me, Sarah and her dad, and off we went to church. I wasn't well established with my faith yet. I hoped the children could learn some truths from Sunday school. I started buying children's Christian magazines for them to enjoy solving the many puzzles they had. I also bought the children's Bible for each of Sarah's older companions. I used to give them two-pound coins each. One to keep and one for collection. I thought of my dad every time I gave out the coins. Wilson's dad would bring Wilson to my flat early on Sunday morning, all dressed up nice and his hair jelled. Michelle and Richard would be already downstairs in the playroom. As we walked to church, we looked like a proper middle-sized family. Once or twice, we had water balloons dropped on us from the flats above. I didn't give it much thought. But why did it happen only on Sundays? Whoever the culprits were, did they know we were going to church? A few drops of water would have never stopped me from going to church. This incident brought to mind the many hardships I had to endeavour during my childhood for being Christian. The one which stuck on my mind is when I was hit by a huge stone. I was probably five or six years old. My next-door neighbours were Christians. We were five families in total living next to each other. It was during the celebration of the Exaltation of the Holy Cross when the True Cross which Jesus was crucified on was found by Saint Helena, the mother of Emperor Constantine. I always loved the name Helena as it is my mother's name. We would gather in a little public garden at the end of the terrace where our houses were situated. We would light a bonfire. My dad would make a swing using a thick rope and hang it on a huge tree nearby. All the kids and the adults would have a turn on the not so comfortable swing. People living in the areas around us knew we were Christian families. We were identifiable by all. On that night, we were showered with stones from where the railway lines were. With the stones, we were hit by came all sorts of verbal abuse. One of those stones hit my left arm. Others were hit too but being a child, I was only concerned about my arm. We had to abandon the celebration and went home.

I applied for a job at the university, and I got it! The job offer brought with it a bittersweet experience and a painful dilemma. Sarah needs to be looked after while I am at work. I found a local nursery for Sarah, which was run by two middle-aged ladies. I had no choice. I tried so many other places and made more than thirty phone calls, desperately looking for a nursery place for Sarah. As I was married, for city council staff, I didn't tick a box. I was living happily with my husband; another box did not get ticked. Was Sarah suffering from any mental health issues? Of course not; another box was not ticked. Has she been referred by her GP for certain anxieties? No, yet again another box was left blank. The conclusion was because I was not a single parent, I had provided a loving and caring home for my child, and she did not suffer any negligence or abuse or whatever; therefore, she was not a priority.

Leaving Sarah at the nursery was tough. The first few weeks were the hardest as I had never left Sarah in someone else' care. I managed to negotiate with my boss so that I started work at 7:30 am and left at 3:30 pm in order to shorten Sarah's time at the nursery. Her dad looked after her in the morning and dropped her off, and I picked her up in the afternoon.

During the following months, I got to know Janet and her husband John really well. She was like a big sister to me. Janet had a beautiful smile and a laid-back nature. When you looked at her, you would think life couldn't faze her. She knew what to do and what to say. She would make comments or give you advice without being forceful or too emotionally involved.

Everything was so effortlessly talked about. She had a cat, which every dog entered Janet's flat was scared of. The cat would chase any visiting dog until it became stuck at the far end of Janet's kitchen. The cat will then stand there staring at the dog as if to say, 'Don't you dare move.'

Janet was in her late forties. She was a white person from South Africa, so she would share with me how hard it was for her at times to be an immigrant from South Africa. Janet had nothing to do with the problems the country was experiencing with the Apartheid and all the publicity which was going on during the early nineties. Sometimes she would hear people making snide comments in her local pub. Janet had a brother living in South Africa. She showed me once a black and white photo of her taken on the ship, which brought her all the way from South Africa to Scotland over thirty years ago.

The following year, Janet's husband, John, got diagnosed with lung cancer. I didn't know much about the disease, and as it was 1991, mobile phones were not born yet, and the internet did not exist, so I couldn't get more information about the disease instantly as we do nowadays. I was full of admiration for Janet for the way she cared for John. She kept him at home, and with the support of other community health workers, she looked after John in the comfort of his home till he passed away. I don't think Janet knew how to cope with the loss of her husband. She grieved for him for a while in her own way. He was everything for her. She looked lost without him. Janet stopped caring for herself and for her daughter Michelle. It was as if she ran out of care ingredients the minute John died. One good thing that came out of this was the insurance money she received after John's death. It wasn't much but enough to pay for a journey to South Africa. Janet visited her childhood neighbourhood, and she spent some time with her brother. It must've been some journey. She showed me the many pictures she took while she visited all the places which, for so long, she had dreamt of going back to.

The weeks and months which followed were a terrible period in Janet's life. It was the start of the end for her. Her flat became a place for consuming alcohol and drugs. Men, some of who were close friends of John, would regularly be present in her flat. The only way I could describe these men was they were vultures. They must've known she had some money left from the insurance, and so rather than going to the local pub, they congregated in Janet's flat. I never saw Janet sober after this period. I would hate to judge other people, but it disturbed me how she was once treated by a member of the paramedic team in one of their visits to her flat. She was awake but totally out. I went to see her when I saw the paramedics in the corridor. The staff member had the attitude of as if she didn't matter. It almost sounded like "here we go again" or "not you again". He was so rough with the way he handled her and moved her from her bed to the stretcher.

Janet was vacant all the time and lost in her inner being in a world of her own. You couldn't get through to her as she wasn't there. There was no way back for Janet. She had lost John, and she had lost herself. Michelle had moved out to live with her brother. Much later in time, I found out Michelle's brother was actually her dad. Matthew was a teenager when his ex-girlfriend got pregnant with Michelle. When Michelle was born, her mother didn't want to look after her neither did Matthew. Janet and John became Michelle's adopted parents, unofficially. Michelle and Matthew's visits to Janet stopped while the visits of many mindless filthy men continued. They will stay up all night, with music blaring all night long. I guessed she would be sleeping during the day. This went on for weeks and months.

One day I came back from work, and as I was at my front door trying to get the keys from my handbag, Janet came out of her flat, not sure what for. She saw me and stood at her flat door, and I stood at my flat door. We were probably fifteen metres away. We didn't say anything. She was totally drunk or on drugs, yet she recognised me, or so I thought. All my love and compassion for her was in my eyes. I so yearned to hold her like my child and take her to my house and look after her. She looked down and slowly turned around and went inside her flat. I stood there for a few minutes, sighing, looking at the spot Janet occupied a minute ago. Should I wait longer in case she came out? Should I go after her? Should I talk to someone about this? As my flat door was now opened, I went inside. What did she want to say? What did she do when she went inside? What went inside her head? Did she take more of whatever stuff to blank out the outside world? I felt hopeless and helpless. I prayed. The kind of prayer with no words but tears, sighs, and question marks but no questions. I hated what her life became, and I hated where I was, not knowing what the solution is.

The loud music continued every night. One night I woke up with Witney Houston's song, *I Will Always Love You*, being played on a loop all night long. My bedroom shared the wall with Janet's bedroom, so I moved to the living room, and I started praying this time for my family and me. I resigned to the fact of what was going on in Janet's flat I couldn't fix. She was destroying herself; these men didn't care, her family abandoned her, was it time for me to admit defeat? I turned to my God, and this time my prayer was simple. 'Please, Lord God, I don't know what to do. If this place is not for me, then please take me away from here. I can't bear it any longer.'

Life couldn't continue like this. I was torn between my inabilities to pull Janet out from her dark world and my patience, which was running out. Every day Janet's world was getting further away from mine. The company she was enjoying, I could not waste a minute with. I was not judging anybody, but they thought they were having a good time. This was not what I consider as having a good time. The woman was grieving, and they were taking advantage of her situation. Pigs, vultures, just pure horrible individuals with no conscious or heart. Did I give up on Janet? Could I have persevered a bit longer?

One night, I went on my knees. I got my Bible out, and I said, 'Please Lord, speak to me, what shall I do?' I was so desperate for God to guide me through his Word. Humanely I could not function, having been up all night with the persistent sad noise and going to work in the morning. I opened my Bible on the page where the scripture read:

Jesus Comforts His Disciples

"Do not let your hearts be troubled. You believe in God; believe also in me. [2] My Father's house has many rooms; if that were not so, would I have told you that I am going there to prepare a place for you?[3] And if I go and prepare a place for you, I will come back and take you to be with me that you also may be where I am. [4] You know the way to the place where I am going."

I felt at peace. It was like someone switched off all the noise inside and outside my head, and all went quiet. And a huge amount of water was poured on me. I closed my eyes and worshiped. I said to myself with full conviction, 'It is time to move house.' The next morning, I shared my thoughts with Ray. He agreed, and we started looking for our first property to buy.

I never saw Janet again. Every time she came to my mind, my heart crunched like a piece of paper. Many years later, it was such a random incident when I was on the phone with a local council department in a different county. The person who answered the phone was Janet's daughter in law. She recognised me when she asked for my name, so we started talking and asking for each other's family, and so I asked how Janet is. She paused for a minute, and then she said: 'Oh, you haven't heard then; I am sorry to say, but Janet was found dead in her flat several months after John had died. She died alone. She must've been dead for weeks, and nobody knew. Apparently, she was buried by the local council.' It was my turn to be quiet. Not much was said after, and the phone call ended. I thought of Janet, my brain rapidly scanning all her images at the times when we first met all the way towards the end of being neighbours. I felt loss mixed with guilt and sadness. The way Janet left this world was never the end, which I would've anticipated for the happy lady with a beautiful smile when I first met her. I had never heard before of the local council replacing the family and friends to bury a person, no funeral service, nothing. I wonder what happened to all the friends who used to circle around her night after night drinking till the early hours of the morning. They left her in her hour of need, just like I did.

Fifteen years later, one day Wilson, now a dad, was pushing his child's pram in a supermarket. He saw Ray, and he recognised him, so he went and spoke with him. I suppose Wilson must've changed a lot, and Ray probably looked the same, only with more grey hair, so he was easier to identify than the all-grown-up Wilson. Wilson asked for me, and he said to Ray, 'I always wondered what had happened to Sarah and her mum.' It is a shame though Ray didn't say to Wilson that I too always wondered what had become of him and the other two little friends. Being men, Ray and Wilson didn't exchange phone numbers, so I never had the chance to see Wilson. I once went to the high-rise building to see if I could see Michelle. The entry to the building was changed and modernised, and so if you didn't have the security card, you couldn't get in. However, I did manage to speak to the caretaker of the building. He knew Michelle. She was with a son, and she had changed her surname. I didn't get to see her as there was no reply from her flat when the caretaker tried to contact her. I never knew where Richard ended up in life. I hope it was in God's plan our paths had crossed for a short period of time. I pray for the three of them will seek Him one day, the source of all comfort.

Ray and I went to see the first-ever home we owned. I loved it the minute we walked in. There were Bible verses on various walls. It had three double bedrooms, so well designed and spacious and, of course, it had a garden. We went to view the house on Thursday, and on the following Tuesday, the house was ours.

So, it was time to prepare for moving the furniture from the flat to the new house. As Ray was very busy with his work, it was down to me to contact the removal companies. One thing I didn't mention about living on floor 17 flat is there were two lifts in the building; however, they didn't stop on each floor. You would have to go to the floor above and then use the stairs for going down to your floor. I never thought about how inconvenient it is going to be for the removal company. I stored our home content in probably 15 big boxes, filled mainly with Ray's books, a fridge-freezer, the living room suite, and a coffee table plus clothes and Sarah's toys. I got the yellow pages and managed to get a quote from a local removal company. One of their staff came to visit the flat and inspected the amount of furniture and boxes we had and based on that I was given an estimate. Since the price was reasonable, we agreed on the time and date of moving house. This person never touched the boxes, so he didn't know how heavy they were as they were filled with books. Trying to be kind, I took some of the books out of each box and filled another probably five smaller boxes with books and topped them with toys.

So, the day of moving the furniture to the new house arrived. We had the keys to our first bought house, and it was a Friday. The removal company would come at 10:00 am. I had arranged for Sarah to spend the day with Jackie and Richard, a couple we knew from the local church. They had a little girl at Sarah's age to play with. There were no mobile phones, of course, in those days. We also had arranged for the landline phone in the flat to get disconnected at mid-day. I stayed in the flat waiting for the removal company to arrive and Ray was in the new house waiting for the furniture to arrive. Jim Watson is another dear friend of ours, who Ray met when he first moved to the city, before Sarah and I joined him.

I was in the flat, waiting impatiently. Two men from the removal company did arrive but late. Their excuse was they were doing another job prior to this one in another part of the city. As I was under their mercy, I asked myself a question but not them: 'Why would they give a certain time and then squeeze another job?' Also, to make matters worse, one of the lifts wasn't working. The two workers knew about the lift as they told me about it when they came to the flat. They counted the boxes, and they said you have five extra. I explained the reason for the extra five was to make the rest less heavy for them to carry. I added, 'I am more than happy to pay extra money for these boxes.'

He said, 'No, we are not taking them; we are contracted to take the 15 boxes, but you will need to phone the office and ask them if they will agree for us to lift the extra boxes.' I told them the phone in the flat was disconnected since mid-day, but I will go very quickly to one of the neighbours and phone the office. When I came back, they had gone. So, I stood there, not knowing what to do. By now, it was half-past four on a Friday afternoon; most places will be shut for the weekend. I panicked. I wanted to focus on what is on hand and what to do next. Sarah will get dropped off soon. Ray is five miles away, waiting for the removal company with his brother and Jim. They would be hungry, of course. Being men, I don't think they would've thought about food. So, I took a taxi and got dropped off on the main road where the new house was. I went to the supermarket, which was on the main road, and bought fruits, drinks, cold meat and salad to make sandwiches. The first expected question as I got in the new house was 'Where is the removal van?' I replied with my relaxed voice.

'It has been delayed a bit but let us eat first.' Nobody objected to my suggestion. Once we finished our sandwiches,

I explained the kind of day I had. My God was listening and watching as I was not alone. His answer came instantly.

Ray so calmly, so unlike him, said, 'It is Friday afternoon these workers were only thinking about the pub calling them with a nice cold pint of lager waiting for them.'

Our dear friend Jim said, 'I know a Christian friend, who works for a Christian charity, and he has a van which he uses to take furniture donated by those who don't need it and take it to those who needed it.' So, Jim made the SOS call. His friend, Eric, answered and he was available, so was the van.

The goodness didn't stop there as Eric said, 'I am going to bring with me a friend of mine to help.'

During this time, Richard – the person who had Sarah staying in their house during the day – arrived to drop Sarah off. When he learnt of what had happened, he offered to stay and help. So, there were Ray and his brother, Richard, Jim, Eric and his friend so within an hour and instead of having two grumpy removal company workers, I had six happy men moving the furniture. The van my furniture was transported in was not an ordinary removal company van, but it had a big beautiful picture on the side with writing below it which read: "Jesus is the light of the world."

Once the furniture was in, we had some more to eat and drink. This time it was more like a prayer and worship time. Jim is a pastor, and his desire to share the Word of God is unstoppable. The Bible verse which the Lord spoke to me with and gave me the sign for moving house was the same scripture which Eric was saved through. This was the second time I witnessed a grown-up man with tears, my dad on my wedding day and Eric as he shared with us his story of how God reached out to him and saved him from the pit he was wasted in. What man wanted to destroy my soul with, with my God it turned into an amazing event where were worshiped and praised Him. I was transported into my new dwelling with a banner which said, "Jesus is the light of the world." What an entrance to the next stage of my life.

Chapter 11

Moulin Terrace

Sarah was three years old when we moved to Moulin terrace. Having a little garden for Sarah to play in was crucial. We replaced the rented flat on floor 17 with an owned upper cottage flat with a little garden. In the evening of the first day at Moulin terrace, Sarah and I went to the back garden, dug the soil out and picked the first big, fat and juicy worm we found. This was Sarah's first pet. A little Tupperware box became the little worm's accommodation for the night. Ray helped in making a few holes in the lid for the air to flow in and out the box. Sarah filled the box with soil, grass and a little bit of water. Neither Sarah nor I touched the worm. It was so satisfying to watch the sheer joy on Sarah's face while caring for her pet while chatting away. The worm with her house was neatly placed on top of the coffee table in the middle of the living room for the night. A few times, I had hated my child mentality mode when I got immersed in child playtime. This was one of them as I caused the death of a creature. I know I had good intentions, but unfortunately, our silly pet time resulted in an unwelcomed outcome. I am not sure what I was expecting to see when I opened the box to check on the worm first thing in the morning. The worm didn't look anything like the plump juicy being we had dug out the night before. It had turned into a thin, stiff thing and dead, of course. Without thinking, the Tupperware and its content was placed in a carrier bag and swiftly buried at the bottom of the big grey rubbish bin behind the house. During the day, when Sarah asked for her pet, I had to explain to her that the worm should stay in the garden, her real home. Trusting as she always had been, Sarah accepted my motherly wisdom with no fuss. This unsettling experience was never repeated.

However, it did bring to mind a more sinister practice I had had to commit when I was at primary school. The teacher had asked the class to bring the skeleton of a frog! Honestly, what was she thinking? My girls were shocked when I shared with them this unpleasant experiment. I must've consulted my siblings then as to how to achieve this. The procedure was to put a frog in a deep bucket and then pour boiling water over it. I am so sorry, my reader, I didn't know any better. However, the sounds the little creature made have haunted me since. It did not stop there as I had to carefully separate the skin and what was underneath from the bones to end up with the dreaded skeleton. I wish I could wipe this horrible tale from my mind, but it has kept annoyingly buzzing in my conscience ever since.

Ray couldn't walk to work from Moulin Terrace as it was probably five miles away. Although financially we could've done without the expense of owning a car and sent the money to our families, however, travelling by public transport wasn't an option. We started looking for a second-hand car. Soon we found the one. It was metallic blue in colour, electric windows, power steering, air conditioning, and it had very low mileage. The car owner was a pensioner whose use of the car was for driving to the supermarket and back.

Ray is an excellent driver for manoeuvring and understanding the mechanics of a car but driving brings the worst in him. It seems as if all the bad drivers come out in the streets when he is driving. Being the oldest son, he was the first to learn to drive, and consequently, he taught his younger siblings how to drive. I am so glad I wasn't inside the car when he imparted his knowledge to his siblings. Being a competent driver is one thing but driving on roads you have never seen before was another thing. He had to learn how to get from home to work. Driving proved to be a huge and stressful experience. During the weekend, we ended up doing the journey from home to work seven times until he knew exactly how to get there without the need for the street maps.

I always felt guilty for not giving Sarah a younger sister or a brother. Sarah was five and a half years old when Rebecca was born. This was not my choice, but it was life's choice for me. However, the neighbours across from us in Moulin Terrace had a daughter called Gillian. Gillian was four years older than Sarah. She was the youngest of three siblings. Although her two older brothers were loving and good to her, I think Gillian enjoyed Sarah's company more. She would play with Sarah as an older sister would. Gillian was almost part of our family. A visit to the Disney store would include Gillian, so did the various trips to country parks. Gillian had the nature of a saint, and I believe she had positively influenced Sarah's growing up. She even taught her how to tie her shoelaces when I failed miserably.

When Sarah started primary school, she was greeted by Gillian and her friends at the entrance of the school. Gillian made Sarah's first day at school a much bearable experience for both Sarah and me. Most of my motherly mistakes happened with Sarah because I didn't know any better. You have to remember I didn't go to a primary school in Britain. Although school is a school no matter what country you are in, however, there were things other mothers knew about, but apparently, I didn't. Sarah's first day was captured on my little camera the same way I did years later with Rebecca's and Rachel's first day at school. Whatever I learnt during Sarah's childhood, the other two sisters benefited from. I had taken Sarah shopping to pick her school uniform, new shoes, school bag, and stationery. Sarah wanted a bright pink coat, which made her look like a little pink riding hood. She wanted bright pink shoes to match. All Sarah's classmates had on a maroon school blazer with black shoes, but not my Sarah. She loved how she looked even more as she was the only primary one pupil with pink shoes and a pink coat. I was oblivious to this as it didn't hit me then how Sarah's pink colour stood out. It pleased her, and so it pleased me. I was thankful for Sarah's teachers, as none of them ever said a word. Sarah got her school's maroon blazer the following year. Recently, when Sarah and I were talking about her first day at school, she said with a big beautiful childlike smile, 'I loved my pink shoes. I would be walking, but constantly, I would be looking down at my beautiful shoes.'

By now, Ray had got used to driving, so I suggested if he could take us for a day out. I found a great adventure park with water rides and other amazing rides I knew Sarah and Gillian would love. The place was out in the country, and the scenery was simply stunning. There were trees to climb and nature corners which various small animals were kept. There was also a nature path where you would walk along an elevated manmade wooden path. It was up at the height of the smaller trees. It felt like you were visiting the trees and be one with nature.

Ray was always against any outings, even if it was to the top of the road and back. Asking him to drive us to the land of the unknown, and with no satellite navigation systems invented yet, was simply a big ask. He did agree at the end. Sarah and Gillian were in the back seats, and I was on the passenger seat with the road atlas on my lap directing Ray. The journey was probably an hour and a half drive each way. Ray was in a good mood at the start of the journey. The happy spell did not last long. We got lost. And, of course, it was always my fault. We kept going around and around, not knowing where the flaming exit was. Ray got impatient and a bit rude to my liking. The first thing he would say in a situation like this: 'What is wrong with the local swing park? Why do we have to come all this distance just for a park?' Then it dawned on him that there would be a cost involved, so he continued, 'God knows how much the entry fee will be for the four of us.' His mouth kept spouting thoughtless and hurtful words. He got even madder when he found out we were running out of petrol. A quick change of plan, we forgot about the park as we had to find a petrol station. Having Sarah and Gillian in the back of the car, I couldn't hold my tears any longer, so I cried silently. I went quiet, and somehow Ray managed to find the petrol station. As Ray was going to pay for the petrol, I asked the girls to come along to pick ice cream and sweets from the petrol station shop. As Ray was paying for the petrol, he asked the lady at the till for direction to the park. Apparently, we were only a few minutes' drive away.

She then said, 'I have free tickets for a family of four; please make use of them.' I looked at her with a timid smile but feeling very grateful. We all thanked her very much.

On the way back to the car, I said to Ray, 'Don't be surprised where and how God would show up.'

He said, 'I know.' He apologised for losing his temper. The rest of the day was amazing. We had a wonderful time, including Ray.

The flats in Moulin Terrace faced identical ones as they were separated by a narrow road. My living room was directly facing the living room of the flat opposite mine. If I was standing at my living room window, I could easily start a conversation with the neighbour across the road with no need for raising my voice. One day, there was a terrible piece of news about a horrific car accident that involved four cars. It happened near the Clyde Tunnel. A car which was driven by a young male driver had left the tunnel and went out of control on a corner. The car then hit the traffic reservation in the middle of the dual carriageway, and careered into traffic from the opposite direction, and ended up on its roof over an incoming car. Inside that car was a young mother and her toddler. They both died instantly. The mother and the child were the daughter-in-law and the granddaughter of my neighbour who lived in the flat across from mine. My neighbours were a nice couple in their late fifties. Although not many of us had met their son and his young family, we all felt their pain. The whole neighbourhood was in shock.

During the day, I was sitting on the sofa in my living room. I stood up to go to the kitchen, and I saw a younger-looking man in the flat across from mine. He was standing at the wide-opened living room window, head down, covering his face with his hand. I sat down back on the sofa as if someone from above pushed me down with a heart-rending sigh and a thought came to my mind. I said to myself, 'Oh no, he must be the person who lost his wife and his little one today.' I sat on the sofa, speechless with my heart aching for him. I stayed away from the living room to give the grieving man his privacy. At times like these, I could only say silent prayers and lots of them. I was not sure how do people live during these times. How did they function? What went into their mind? How did they get over this pain and loss? I couldn't sleep that night. I kept bringing my neighbour's son to my God, asking Him to pour His love and comfort over the grieved man. I wanted to give my neighbour a card, but I didn't know what words to put down. Words could be soothing and comforting, yet I knew whatever words I came up with would've been meaningless. For my neighbour's son, and on that specific day, everything was meaningless.

I was restless all night. Tossing and turning and pleading with my Father above. I started arguing with God on behalf of my neighbour. There are situations in life you, as a mere human being, just don't have answers. What do you do? Your mind melts down, and your senses become muddled. You go through the now and here, and yet one incident has turned your world upside down. How was this man going to enter his flat and enter each room and still standing! No wife and no child for no fault of his own. Why him? Why like this? How did you expect him to survive? That morning there were three of them, but on the afternoon of the same day, there is only him.

By now, it was after three o'clock in the morning. I got up and sat in the corner of the sofa, the spot which my God had shown me many visions, including the one about Princess Diana's death, another one about Ray's amazing project for building a temple for the Lord and seeing in advance the person who was to assassin Israel's Prime Minister. I was tired of asking questions. I opened my Bible and put it on my lap. I prayed earnestly and said, 'Please, Lord God, I have no words of mine to ease this man's pain. Please give me your words. Please, Lord, give me words that will comfort this man through this dark time.' I opened my Bible, and there in front of me were the words from the book of Isaiah, chapter 57, verses 1 and 2. Words which I had never come across before.

"The righteous perish, and no one ponders it in his heart; devout men are taken away, to be spared from evil. Those who walk uprightly enter into peace; they find rest as they lie in death."

I got a card and wrote a few words explaining myself, and then I wrote the scripture and signed the card. First thing in the morning, I put the card through the letterbox as I wanted to make sure this man gets the card in case he was going back to his flat. My prayer was for His words to turn what was meaningless into meaningful. There are times when only God can do. This day was one of those times. I never saw that man again, and I would not recognise him if I see him today. I don't know what he made of the words in that card. Words that until that day I didn't know existed. Words that were meant for the grieving husband and father. Despite his pain, I hoped he would hold on to the words, "they enter peace". Humanly there was nothing I could've done. I prayed, got the words, delivered the words, and I left it to the Author of words and life to sort out.

Years later, my niece shared with me a dream she had about dying. The word of God says death will happen so fast, like a twinkling of an eye. My niece described the death as, 'Imagine you had your house coat on hanging on your shoulders, but you don't have your arms through its sleeves. You lie down on your back, stretching your body on your bed with your housecoat spread under your body. When we die, it is like you get up from your bed, leaving the housecoat on your bed. Your housecoat is basically your earthly corpse which you leave behind.' Missing the departed by those left behind is what makes death sting. Otherwise, for the believers, death is the end of a turbulent journey to reach home.

Chapter 12

I Am One of Them

While working at the university, I was part of a team of six researchers, two admin support, and a team leader. We were attached to the university, but we were housed in a building off Byres Road. It was a great place, a beautiful huge Victorian building. It used to be a family house in the past, imagine that. In order to get to my work, I had to catch a bus, walk to the subway station and get the subway to Hillhead stop. I hadn't had my driving licence yet. After seven years, we were told there would be no more funding available for our unit. Our project had reached the conclusion stage. Obviously, we were all devastated. We had three months' notice. We were the victim of our own success as the training we provided centrally now it was being offered locally.

Rebecca was not a year old yet. We had bought our first house at Moulin Terrace. This meant a large sum of money went towards paying off the mortgage. I am not conceited, but I know myself I couldn't rely but on Him for my daily bread. I simply couldn't live not having the money that I have earned. I never liked money, and I never will. What I get, I give away, but at the same time, I cannot rely on any other person for money, not even Ray. I would do any job but not ask for money. I was really puzzled. I know my God knows my needs before I do. I didn't get it. Why would my God allow for this to happen? After leaving work that day, and as I came out of the subway station, it was dark, and it was bucketing with rain. The type of rain with big and heavy drops which burst into a big splash once they hit the ground. I walked to the bus stop. Even if there was one person standing in the bus shelter, it would've been one person too many. I needed space. I didn't want to see anybody or anything. If only I could've magically erased everything around me. My feet made the decision this time once again, and so instead of staying in the bus shelter, I started walking. My feet didn't think of how I would then sit on a bus seat if I was to catch a bus soon, with clothes dripping with water. I kept walking. I skipped the following bus stops and continued walking. The rain was so heavy it felt like I was being lashed with tree branches. I ended up walking all the way home. And all the way home, I was crying bitterly and loudly like a child.

As it was dark and cold, I knew nobody would notice or hear me. Nobody would be daft enough to be walking in such weather. I kept saying to myself and to my God, 'I just can't lose my job. I can't. I just can't lose my house.' I kept talking to my God the whole journey home. It did not make any sense to me. I was asking myself, 'Why would God give me this job, and then He would take it away from me? Why would He give me a house, and the next minute He takes away my salary? My Father above doesn't do this. My Father only gives.'

Although it was a long walk, I wished it never ended. I didn't want to go home. In fact, I didn't want to go anywhere. I didn't know how to share my bad news with Ray. I had learnt that I have to prepare Ray before I share with him certain subjects. This one was one of these subjects. I had to spare myself from hearing the wrong words. So, although it felt like I had a cold and very long shower, yet I was boiling inside with heat that could have melt anything. Yet the rain which hit me didn't turn into steam. I felt injured; every part of me inside and out was broken. God is good. My God is not just good; He is great. I started asking Him, 'I know you are seeing, hearing, feeling all of this, so please tell me what to do?'

Although walking in the rain sounded a daft idea, but by the time I got home, I felt my soul was at such peace. It was such a therapeutic workout, and I would recommend it to anybody. I didn't share my bad news with Ray that night. I did though when I was ready. It was like a counselling session for Ray. He is a darling; however, I need to explain things to him with examples. Give him solutions before I talk to him about problems.

While I was still working at the university, I started looking for a job. Soon I had a job interview at one of the other universities in the city, but I was not successful. Weeks after, I was offered three jobs at the same time. I needed to choose one of them. So, I did. I chose the one my Heavenly Father chose for me. How do I know? Well, here is how. I had applied for a job as a lecturer in a Further Education (FE) college, a community college. I didn't know much about the cohort of learners I would be teaching. The campus was 20 miles drive each way from my house. And I had just passed my driving test. As a matter of fact, when I posted the application form for the job, I wasn't a driver yet, but I was sitting the driving test shortly after. So, it happened between posting the application form and getting the job interview that I received my driving licence. Despite having my official driving instructor, however, my best friend Valerie's many hours of teaching me didn't go to waste. She was so pleased for me as if she herself received a second driving licence.

Days prior to the job interview, I had rediscovered the meaning of rainbow as I was studying the story of Noah. Since then, whenever there was a chance of a rainbow appearing in the sky, I would take my time to fill my eyes with its beauty and fill my mind with its meaning. I would whisper, 'I love my Lord, and I know you love me.' I would hear myself repeating the word "wow" as I keep looking at the rainbow until it faded away. On the day of my job interview, I was well prepared. I had a skirt suit on. It was a light green colour with a beige, gold top. I know I looked smart. I had printed my slides in colour and on shiny sheets. In those days, this was very advanced technology. While driving on my way to the job interview, I was earnestly seeking my Father's opinion. 'Please give me a sign that this is where you want me to be.'

You could imagine how overwhelmed I was when while I was seeking, through loud prayer, an amazing rainbow appeared on the side of the road. There were many farms I passed by, nature at its best, green, green and more green grass and trees and a golf course or two. The dual carriageway was winding at times. This rainbow was so different and unique. It wasn't an arch, but it was like a wide column, a heavenly shape rather than a rainbow. I was transformed totally into a worship state in awe and wonder. I honestly don't know how I was driving, not to mention I was a new driver. This heavenly shape was so intense in colour. It was on the right-hand side of the road, but I couldn't take my eyes off it. I knew my God was in communication with me. So, like a child chatting to her loving father, I said: 'Am I going to get this job?' So, before I finished the question, the road changed direction, so the rainbow was facing me; it was in front of me, blinding me with its intense and vivid colours, so wide, so awesome. I am not sure how I managed to drive the car, but I continued driving. I felt the column inside my car. It was like the roof of the car had disappeared to make way for the rainbow to enter my car. I had never experienced anything like it before. I felt the heat of it inside the car. It was simply supernatural moments that I would treasure forever. I felt so calm and at peace as if I was floating in heaven. I went to the job interview with full confidence appreciating my Father's gift and His presence.

As time passed, I would discover new perks about this job, more amazing reasons why my God picked it for me. It was a full time, permanent post, and I was put on top scale or grade for salary from day one. After starting my job, I came to know my job contract was offered for the first time. Apparently, when employed, you had to go through a part-time contract first, working in the community, perhaps doing evening classes. Many years later, and only then, you might get offered a full time and permanent post. I also had a 25% pay rise compared to my previous job. Instead of only having 30 days annual leave for this new job, I had 64 days. My starting date was in the middle of April. I was asked if I was willing to start earlier and cover classes, so I said yes. A holiday was due from my work at university. For what was my last month at my old job and my first month in the new job, I had two salaries plus the overtime for covering classes. I also received a cheque with thousands of pounds because apparently losing my job meant I was made redundant; therefore, I was due payment. At the end of the month, I had so much money in my bank account I had never had before. It didn't stop there. The scenery in Scotland is simply stunning. Driving to work and enjoying the beauty of God's creation, I would remind myself I was going to work and not on a day trip. Also, the cars in the other direction were every day stuck in a traffic jam, unlike mine. It was the same story going back home. I did my duties at work with the mind of knowing my God was my employer; therefore, every lesson I gave, every conversation I had, every situation I had to deal with, I did it with Him, and for Him, to honour Him and to show Him my gratitude.

With the new job, I needed a car. I bought one, a little bright blue Rover. It was a struggle to drive the car up the hill on the motorway. I was always on the left lane, the slow lane, as I couldn't go faster than any other car. Every other car overtook me, of course. I would look at the front mirror, I would see a car behind me, only for a while though. Soon, it was racing on my right, and in a few minutes, it would disappear in the distance. If there was to be a race on the motorway, I would always come last. In my defence, I am a safe driver. I don't just comply with the speed limit when passing a traffic speed camera or when a police van is hiding to catch speeding drivers. When I was young, we used to watch a motoring programme on television. The presenter used to always end his programme with the same few words to remind his viewers 'driving is art, skill and good manners.' However, I couldn't blame my slow driving on the little Rover. To the annoyance of everybody on the road, I turned out to be a slow but safe driver.

My little Rover didn't have any of the nice features Ray's car had. Every time I had a shot at driving Ray's car, I hated mine. Trying to do a three-point turn was such a workout I was always out of breath at the end of it. How did the drivers manage in the past without power steering? One day I noticed a dent in the back of Ray's car. Although the damage was confined to a small area, and it didn't look good. It was too deep, but no rips or anything like that. Ray had reversed into a short concrete pole without noticing it. I suggested we took the car to a local garage to have it fixed. We were given a £400 estimate for repairing the dent. Fixing it through an insurance company was not an option as Ray didn't want to lose no claims bonus. £400 would pay for one of our siblings' rent in Jordan for three months. We resigned to postpone the repair to the near future. The dent was like an eyesore, and if only I had a magic wand to make it vanish.

If I caught Ray while he was in a good mood and asked him nicely, he would agree to switch cars. So, it happened one day he was in a good mood, and he did let me drive his car to work. What could go wrong? I had driven the same route for months by then, and we had a good spacious car parking facility at work. I loved driving Ray's car as it didn't struggle on the motorway at the hilly bit.

Driving through the beautiful scenery on my way to work, never ceased to amaze me. In all seasons, the scenery is always beautiful, always awesome. With every glance at the beautiful nature, the more I realised how unique every element was. There were no two identical trees. The sky changed every moment. When I intensely inspected the clouds, their ever-changing shapes, their various shades of white and greys, it simply was free astonishing art in front of me to enjoy. No artist in history could compete with the scenes in the sky. The drive to work made my day even before arriving at the college's car park. I would pour out my heart to Him about what was annoying me or upsetting me. A chat with my heavenly Father and surrounded by beautiful nature was like my morning fix. On that particular day, driving Ray's car, just added a bit of luxury to my experience. After exiting the motorway, there was a five minutes' drive before I get to the college's car park. I was at a giveaway sign at a busy junction. My car was stationary, and I was tense, focusing on the traffic and waiting for my turn to join the road to work. All of a sudden, I heard a bang, and my body felt the impact. It was then I knew how a whiplash felt like. It was also my first time ever to be involved in a traffic accident. I sat motionless for a few moments, not knowing what just had happened. The next minute, a man – who was probably in his mid-forties – was standing right next to the driver's door. He was asking me anxiously if I was all right. I said, not sure of anything, 'I think so.' I didn't see any blood anywhere, and apart from my neck, I didn't feel any pain. He kept apologising while trying to explain to me what just happened. He gave me his details and his car details, including the name of his insurance company. He asked me for my name and my telephone number, and he said he would call me today.

He said, 'I have been driving for twenty-five years, and I have never been involved in a car accident.' Apologising again, he said, 'I just didn't see your car.' He continued, 'There was no point in calling the police. I made an error of judgement. As long as you are okay and you can drive your car, it is better to move on and not obstruct the traffic. But please make sure you go to A&E to have your neck checked.'

If you want the definition of a gentleman, then this driver was it.

I continued my journey to work with one question on my mind: "what will I tell Ray?" I looked at the back of the car, and it looked bad. Still, life is more precious than any metal.

Throughout the day, I couldn't stop sensing the impact of the incident over and over again. I was shaking inside. I guessed it was my body's way of getting over the unexpected and the sudden hit. During the following days and weeks, I was terrified of having any car near behind me. When I arrived home, Ray came to the door and said, 'Are you okay?'

I said, 'Yes, I am fine.' And stopped at that. I didn't need to say more; apparently, the gentleman driver had already phoned home, expressing again how sorry he was, and he had already contacted his car insurance to get Ray's car fixed. It occurred to me then, what about the dent which was already there? I went quiet for a minute, and then it hit me. I said to Ray, 'Does this mean the dent will get fixed? It has to be.' Ray and I had naughty grins on our faces.

There was no point in suggesting to the car insurance company. 'Yes, thank you, but wait, there was an earlier dent.' How on earth they could differentiate the one from the other. And so, although I took the hit, I believe my God used it to get the car fixed for Ray without costing us a penny. Instead, the money went to our families who needed it most. In my heart, I thanked again the stranger who, with an angel's attitude, delivered yet another heavenly message.

One Sunday, while attending my local church, we had a guest pastor preaching on how God can use you no matter where you are and how the place of employment could become your church. Every word I heard spoke to my heart as I was desperate to share God's goodness with my family and me, so I kept talking to my God, asking Him to use me in any capacity. So, I thought I could start the Christian Union in my college!

I picked the yellow pages and looked for the local churches near my college. I needed the help of other fellow believers. I wasn't very confident yet in witnessing God's love and using His word to answer questions from those who might be seeking. I knew Him and His promises and His love in my own way, but I felt I lacked the depth of knowledge of the Bible to be able to stand firm when challenged by other views. It was my God's reputation I had to consider. Was I ready? Was I clear about the commitment I expected of others? Maybe not. So, I phoned the first and the second closest churches to my college and spoke to whoever answered the phone and explained what I was dreaming of and if they would be willing to come to the college and support me to witness to the students. Both phone calls were disappointing, and I was left with a blank mind, disappointed, but I was not giving up. The fire had started in my heart, and I could not stop it. I accepted it wasn't God's time, so I kept dreaming.

The King of glory knew me; He knew my heart. He knew my limitation; He knew my weaknesses and my strengths more than any psychologist. He knew my shortcoming to recite His word when put on the spot. He knew it all, and despite it all, He saw me worthy of sharing His love with my students. So, with His mighty hand, a door was opened for me at the college to witness in a way I never thought it was possible.

One day, and during one of my lessons, and as I usually go around the room checking on students' progress, I overheard one of my students saying while holding to a small tract with a Christian message on: 'Oh, this was given to me by one of these God's squad.' Every time the word God would get mentioned, I would pay attention more than usual as at times I would use it as an opening to share with my students, only if asked, God's love and His plan for our lives.

And if asked, 'Why are you so nice?'

I would reply, 'Do you really want to know?' So, I take the opportunity and sum up the good news in a three to five minutes chat. So, without being intimidating and in a jokey way, I said, 'What is wrong with God's squad? I am one of them.' As I was clearing my classroom after the end of the lesson, collecting any unwanted paper, I noticed the little tract was left behind, not binned, but pushed behind the computer's monitor. I picked it up. It had Bible verses and contact details of a pastor who lived in the town. I got all excited. That little sheet of paper was the key to a wide door being opened for the word of God to be shared and ministered to the students in the college. I couldn't wait to get home to make the phone call. Apparently, instead of one person, I had a team of three wanting to come and compensate for my weaknesses.

I had two young American lady missionaries and a pastor to help me with this privileged service. The group had started a new church in the area, and they had been praying earnestly for a door to be opened to have a presence in the college. A presence was granted. I met with the management of the college seeking permission, and this too was granted. I was given a room which I chose to be on the second floor of the building. We had regular weekly Christian Union meetings during lunchtime. The slot even appeared on my timetable. I was given a discount from the canteen staff for the 12 meals I bought every week. We had a selection of sandwiches, cans of soft drinks, and chocolate bars. These were prepared for me each week by the canteen staff and put in a big brown box. So, we would eat while we shared the word of God, prayed, and sang worship songs. A little version of heaven on the second floor. Imagine the sound of worship songs praising my God and my King and the sound of a guitar playing in the heart of the college. Later on, rather than using a classroom, we moved to the students' common room so we can be more noticed.

At certain times of the year, we organised special events showing Christian movies. We also took the Christmas Carol Services at the college, which used to be an annual celebration attended by both staff and students. One year, before stopping for Easter break, we arranged an event. I asked the canteen staff to make a buffet lunch. There were many trays of food that needed to be carried from the canteen to the big hall where the crowd was gathering. As I turned around to head towards the hall, the senior member of the management team said to me, holding one of these trays, 'So you know I am doing my bit in helping out.' We were going to show the movie, the Passion of the Christ. The lecture theatre was packed with students and staff. I had a guest speaker, a young man from the Scottish Christian Union team who spoke so well, reaching out to the crowd with the message of the Cross and the Resurrection. We showed some of the scenes from the movie, picked carefully. I loved how the speaker talked about the Gospel of John, and he explained how the writer of this gospel had lived for real the scenes which we just finished watching. The speaker made the Scripture become alive to the audience by inviting them to read for themselves what they visually watched. We had lots of copies of John's Gospel to give out. They were re-produced in a format that could appeal to the students. I believe seeds were planted that day, and I trusted the Lord God would have opened the hearts and the minds of those who were seeking.

Chapter 13

Valerie

In life, people have friends and family to support them and share life with them during good times and hard times. I had those, but I also have Valerie. She is so precious she has to have a category of her own. She is to inherit my girls when I die as my girls would say she is their other mammy.

I lived at Moulin Terrace when I met Valerie. I lived on the top flat at the end of a terrace, which meant I shared the back garden with the family living on the ground floor. Valerie's flat and mine were back-to-back. Our flats shared part of the back fence. Her flat was on the ground floor. Before I met Valerie, I used to watch her play with her identical twin boys in the back garden. It astounded me how effortlessly she cared for them, like a first-class mum with supernatural powers. Lewis and Daryl were several years older than Sarah. They both had severe physical and mental disabilities. Lewis and Daryl couldn't utter any proper words to their mother, but Valerie never stopped conversing with them, and at times, of course, singing to them too. She saw them as the best, and she gave them her best. Lewis and Daryl could walk but not for very long distances. She would have the boys out whenever the weather permitted. I bet I wasn't the only mother watching and admiring her parenting skills.

Every time I looked through my kitchen window and saw them, I called out to my heavenly Father and asked him to pour His strength, His peace, and His love for Valerie and the boys. I wished I could meet with her, but I didn't know how to go about it. A few days later, I took Sarah out to the back garden to play. Valerie and the boys were out too. My back garden was longer and narrower than Valerie's. Sarah was playing on the side of the garden, which was further away from Valerie. I strolled to the other end of the long and narrow back garden to fetch Sarah's ball back. Valerie noticed me, and she smiled. We said hello to each other. The warmth which came out from her face would've melted the whole neighbourhood. We stood there chatting away with Sarah and me and including the boys in all the subjects we talked about. At the end of the day, I knew her name, the boys' names, and an exuberant joy filled my heart.

Time went by, and one day Valerie came to my door, and she said, 'Would you like to come to my house? I am having a night in, and I have invited a few ladies.' I was over the moon. Perhaps happier than being invited by the queen to visit her palace. I couldn't wait to have the chance to spend the evening with Valerie and the boys and to get to know them. Little did I know; this was a prayer meeting! Wow, Valerie, and a prayer meeting! She, too, had been praying for me since the first time she noticed me. Imagine that! This was the start of a lifetime journey that both Valerie and I would treasure till we meet again in heaven. Valerie was a child of God. What a joy.

No matter what life threw at Valerie, and no matter what hardship she was going through, each year, each one of my family members would receive a birthday card from Valerie. The girls, of course, were given a gift too. Many years, Ray and I would remember it was our birthday only when a birthday card arrived through the letterbox from Valerie. I, however, did not have the same commitment, yet she always accepted me just the way I am. She always had the right words to say in every situation, whether she was talking to me, Ray, or the girls. She overwhelmed me with the same non-judgemental presence I felt with my mother. Valerie and I meant the world to each other. Seeing her made it all better. She would come, and she would talk, and I would listen, or I would talk, and she would listen, and that was it. We would depart, having been left with the peace and gratitude we had for each other.

Lewis and Daryl could make noises as their way of communicating with their mum, but I know from the look on their faces they enjoyed every word they heard, the soothing words she would say to them. Valerie was their everything, and they were her everything. She was tireless in her nonstop ability to care for her boys. She gave her boys the best quality of life no other mother could have done. Valerie fought for her boys, as fierce as a lioness, and ensured they got the best services available. Their bibs needed to be changed so many times a day, even during the short period of time I was present. I would see the pulley filled with their washed bibs hanged up to dry. And although Valerie had an extra room made as a playroom for the boys, filled with all sorts of toys and musical instruments, the boys' favourite toys were the ones Valerie made for them. To the outsiders, they didn't resemble anything like a toy, but to her boys, they couldn't do without their mother's handmade toys.

Lewis and Daryl were totally dependent on Valerie for every function to survive: eating, walking, and bathing. She would always say: 'It is not their disabilities that break my heart, but it is all the other illnesses and the many allergies which made their lives so much harder.' They constantly needed medical attention. As they grew older, their bodies got stronger, and their immune systems got better. Once their food was all mushed up, she would sit them near her, or even while they had their wee walk in the garden; she would give a spoonful of food to each one of them at a time. Daryl always wanted more, while Lewis was more reluctant in receiving his share of food. It was like, 'Okay, let us get on with this other mouthful.' The same attitude to food like my two youngest girls. Lewis and Daryl needed constant supervision as they were not aware of how little things could harm them. Daryl had a little day trip with the school to attend cookery class in the local college cut short as he picked a raw chicken drummer and put it in his mouth. It is these details other mothers take for granted their children will be safe on their own but not for Valerie. She was their eyes, their ears, their mind, their hands, basically all their senses. Sadly, Valerie lost Daryl when he was 19, and she lost Lewis when he was 26. Until their last day alive, Valerie had to change their nappies. This act of love and care alone would make you wonder how on earth she did it. When they were first diagnosed with their disability, Lewis and Daryl were given by the medical team twelve years to live. No one will ever know or understand the sheer weight Valerie carried throughout her life caring for the boys and sadly grieving for them since she lost them. Lewis and Daryl couldn't utter the words, but I know they were the proudest children for having such a unique and simply outstanding person for a mother.

Valerie and I journeyed this life together. At times we leant on each other, and at other times we danced together. So, although there were the five of us in my family, my God was always number one, making six of us, then there was Valerie, the seventh family member. I also belonged to her family, as one night during a night out, and while we were having a nice meal with her mum and two sisters, Valerie's mum said to me, 'I want to adopt you as my daughter.' This was done unofficially, of course. I didn't know what to say, but I had a big smile on my face.

Valerie had the magic ability to appear at my doorstep instantly whenever we needed the company of each other. When I moved to Moulin Terrace, I was still working at the university. I relied on public transport for all my travels, but it was time I learnt to drive. Soon I started taking driving lessons. My instructor was useless. I suspect he was having health or mental issues, which caused him to be quiet for the whole duration of the lesson. Also, it seemed as if he didn't know the roads very well as he always took me through the same route. I never had a driving instructor before, so I didn't know any better. Until one day, Valerie took me out to drive. It was like a day and night experience. So, she said, 'Get yourself another driving instructor. You are not going to pass your driving test if you stay with this one.' So, I ended up with another driving instructor. Valerie chose a much better one for me. She continued to be my extra driving instructor. Every time I see Valerie, she would tell me how terrible a driver she was. Having to drive with the twins in the back of her car for most of the time, it was God who was driving the car for her. Still, to me, she was the greatest driving instructor.

First Encounter

So, one evening, Valerie came to my door, in need of a break. She suggested we walk to the little coffee shop on the main road, which was a five minutes' walk from our houses. Sometimes I know I can be like a child, an idiot one, excited about little things, and so I said, 'Why don't I drive us?'

Valerie is four ft ten inches, so she said, 'I don't think this is a good idea. If anything happens, I can't drive your car; my feet won't reach the peddles.' I was, I suppose, persistent with a big smile on my face, so she reluctantly agreed. I ran quickly and got the L plates and placed them on the front and the back of the car.

At this point in time, I had learnt moving the car forward, changing gears, driven the car with speed less than 30 miles per hour, but I hadn't practised hill start, I hadn't started any manoeuvres yet, and I definitely hadn't learnt how to reverse the car. To leave our neighbourhood and to get to the main road, I had to drive over a little and narrow bridge. A few months earlier, the local council had made the driving on this bridge a one-way system since the bridge was deemed to be weak. The council had installed a temporary set of traffic lights on each side of the bridge. My car was at the bottom of the road, but further up, the road became steep and hilly. I saw the green light changed to amber. I was planning to continue to drive when I was suddenly instructed by Valerie to stop. And I did. This was followed by a lecture from her. She basically was telling me off, so she said: 'You should always stop when the light changes to amber.' She continued, 'This is not a straight road. You can't see beyond the summit. How can you judge what the drivers from the other side of the road would do?' I knew she was right, so she did the telling off, and I did the taking in. Then her voice sounded more serious and authoritarian, so she said: 'It could be even worse, what if the next car coming from the other side is a police car, then we would both be in real trouble.'

And of course, as I hadn't planned to stop my car when she so abruptly told me to do so, my car was now in the middle of the road. The space on my right would barely fit another car. My car should've been parked right at the edge of the road to allow for the incoming traffic to pass by. So, I said to her, 'I am not sure what to do now.' So, we agreed we wait and see maybe, with a bit of luck, there won't be any incoming cars before we see the green light again. But, of course, there was an incoming car, and of course, it was a police car. So, I panicked, and Valerie panicked even more. When pressed like this, I usually start giggling but not that day. Valerie's voice became louder, and there was more urgency to it.

So, she said: 'You have blocked the way of the police car. Now listen to my instructions and do as I tell you.'

I was too scared to open my mouth, but I had to say to her: 'Val, I am sorry, but you know I don't know how to reverse the car.' She didn't swear because we both oozed with faith; however, she made noises, which sounded like puuuffff, shaking her head with frustration.

There was more. Valerie was the first to admit to having problems with telling her right from her left. And so, for her to direct me to reverse the car under the watchful eyes of the policemen, it was too much to ask of anybody, let alone

Valerie. She told me to turn the steering wheel to the right when it was supposed to be to the left. So, I followed my trusted friend's instruction, and I did reverse the car, as she told me to. If the car was not in the middle of the road earlier, it absolutely was in the middle of the road after my first ever manoeuvre. So, we both panicked more. To make matters worse, she said: 'We are both going to jail.' As she finished her powerful conclusion, to our demise, I saw one of the police officers came out of his car and walked towards us. We just went quiet. I knew how to roll down the driver's window. Neither Valerie nor I had the chance to remember to seek the help of our heavenly Father, but I know he was watching and probably laughing too. I decided not to leave the car to speak to the police officer as I was shaking like a leaf.

Before the police officer said anything, I started apologising and stating the fact I am a learner and how sorry I was. The police officer very calmly said, 'Take your time. It is not a problem.' Then he returned to his car. This time both Valerie and I performed better and managed to get the car better positioned, although I did hit a road sign which was behind me. This was the road sign to warn the drivers about the traffic lights. The police car slowly managed to pass by my car. We didn't look at them, of course. We focused on the road, and neither of us said a word until I started moving the car.

Valerie said: 'I don't believe what just happened. We have been so lucky.' She continued: 'Please, once you drive over the bridge, park the car in the nearest spot you find.'

I said, 'Of course.' I had stopped the car before, but I think with all this pressure and the excitement, I forgot any learning I have acquired about parking, so instead of parking the car on the road, I managed to park the whole car on the pavement. It really wasn't funny. Both Valerie and I knew for any car to drive over the bridge there was one way out from our neighbourhood, which was back over the bridge again. As it took a few minutes to drive around the whole area, this meant anytime now the police car would return. I did earnestly try to follow Valerie's anxious instructions and managed to move the car in the direction she commanded. The car was now at a ninety-degree angle with the road, half of the car on the pavement, and a half on the road. By this point, Valerie had enough. She decided to take charge before the police came back. As we swapped seats, we saw the police car coming towards us again. Valerie pulled the driver seat forward, as far as it could go. With a bit of luck and having stretched her little feet forward, she managed to reach the pedals. In no time, Valerie had the car parked properly, pulling the hand brake so forcefully I thought it would come out. One instruction I should have given her, but I didn't was to press the little button at the end of the hand brake before she pulled it up. She never did. As the police car passed by our car, it didn't stop this time. 'Should we go to the coffee shop?' I said. Valerie looked at her watch, and apparently, she did have some time left.

She replied, 'Aye.' So, we did. As we sat inside the coffee shop, enjoying our hot drinks, it was our turn to laugh at ourselves. We promised each other never to tell our husbands about our little adventure.

Chapter 14

Bluebells

I hate housework. I have repeated this statement to myself, so many times, I have stopped being ashamed of saying it. When I lived in Gipsy Lane in Oxford, I was responsible for washing clothes for the first time in my life. We didn't have a washing machine. The kitchen was too small to accommodate one. We didn't use the local laundrette. Ray was against it. He had seen somebody putting his shoes inside the washing machine, so? This was Ray's excuse, and I was so silly to agree. My hands were not strong enough to squeeze the excess water out. Drying the clothes was a nightmare. I planned this dreaded chore so I would wash a few items at a time and do the washing more frequently. Many a time, when I was in a bad mood, I would bin one or two items. I would decide which ones to throw in a bin; usually, they were Ray's big and heavy items. I chose not to disclose this piece of information to him. Much later in life, and when Ray discovered he didn't mind helping out, he started vacuum cleaning the house. Of course, everybody we knew would've heard about Ray having a bad deal and this extra strenuous chore allocated to him. I thanked him, of course, each time he did it. There was nothing like when the carpet has been hoovered. It was more satisfying than putting makeup on.

To my advance, there came an answer. I have a skin condition. So ironic though, but, in my opinion, is a valid reason, as to why I didn't enjoy housework. My GP gave this condition the name "Housewife Disease". Every time I said this name, I had to stop myself from laughing. When I told Ray this, he said, 'I don't believe you. You have made this up.' Obviously not! Apparently, my hands become very dry when I use them for housework. They still do. And if I was not careful, the skin broke up with cracks like the ones you see on the surface of a land cursed with drought. On extreme occasions, the cracks will start bleeding. If I wanted to do any housework, I had to wear cotton gloves first, after applying lots of specially made moisturising cream on my hands. I would then have to wear a pair of rubber gloves on top of the cotton gloves. I could be excused, in my opinion, if I felt I want to run a mile from the mention of the word housework.

My GP ordered certain blood tests to help diagnose what was causing my skin condition. Although the blood tests confirmed the condition, my GP had another piece of information for me. During the consultation, he said to me, 'I am not sure what your family planning at present is, but I need to let you know that your blood tests showed your ovaries are not producing eggs.' I had only Sarah then. Sarah was five years old. Financially we were totally committed to other higher causes as our extended families were gradually, one by one, immigrating. They relied on the money we use to send home. During the sanctions imposed on Iraq, one-pound sterling was worth a handbag full of Iraqi dinars. Presently having another child, unfortunately, was not a choice. My GP did say though, 'This does not mean you can never be able to have another child. When in the future you think it is the right time for you to have a baby, then come back and see us. You will be given certain treatment, and in most cases, it should work.'

Soon, the time was right as now most of our family members were settled in the countries they chose to emigrate to. This meant I could now think about my own family. I was thirty-four years old, and I wanted another baby; however, I wasn't sure what this treatment was, how long it would take, and most importantly, it would work or not. The night Rebecca was conceived, I was praying silently and so solemnly. I asked: 'Lord, God, if it is Your will, please let me have another child.' I had bitter tears longing for another child. I didn't think much about it in the following days and weeks. I was planning to book an appointment with my GP to find out more about this treatment. My God did hear me that night. I didn't need to go and visit my GP as I was already pregnant with Rebecca. My Rebecca, what a joy, her name means the servant of God.

Rebecca's arrival in this world was so unexpected and almost a passing breeze. It was a Wednesday morning, and I had a team meeting at work at 10:00 am. At 4:00 am, I was tossing and turning, feeling a bit of pain in my tummy. I thought it must be wind, so I went to the bathroom. On the five steps journey to the bathroom, I realised it wasn't the wind that was rumbling in my tummy, but I was in labour. The contractions were fast and became painful. Although Rebecca's due date was in two weeks' time, I had my bag ready. So, I went to wake Ray up. The first thing he said to me, 'How do you know you are in labour?' I have learnt to hear statements like these from Ray and not get annoyed. The next thing, of course, was to phone Valerie. She was at my front door in less than ten minutes.

She said, 'Ray, do you know the way to the hospital?'

'No' was the reply. As Rebecca arrived two weeks earlier, Ray hadn't had the chance to learn the route to the hospital.

So, Valerie said, 'I am going to go and get my car, so I will drive in front of you, Ray.' In the meantime, I had a quick shower, and then I woke Sarah up. Her dad got her school uniform and school bag ready. I had five minutes to explain to Sarah what was happening. Sarah was so excited to become a big sister despite being half asleep. Valerie was back with her car in no time. She put Sarah in the back of her car. Ray followed behind, with me in the back of his car, feeling every pothole he drove over and with a little moan. Valerie disregarded all the red lights as she drove through every set of the traffic lights on the way. Ray followed. We arrived at the maternity building, but the main door was shut. Valerie was definitely in charge. She ran around the building and found a side door that was open. I felt the baby was about to pop out, any minute now. Valerie waved to me where the door was, thinking I could just run to it, but I could hardly stand. Mounting the curb to get to the pavement was such a mammoth ask for a woman with a baby's head just about to appear any minute now. I needed somebody to give me a gentle push from the back. However, we got in, just in time.

Valerie, our hero, took Sarah with her and went home. I was rushed to the labour suite. Not long after, Rebecca's beautiful face graced this world at 6:20 am. My bundle of joy was resting in my arms. With every moment gazing at my brand-new baby and feeling her in my arms, I gave thanks to

Him who made it possible. Having the hospital 20 minutes' drive from home was a blessing, I was immensely grateful for having Valerie in my life.

Since that day, Valerie and Rebecca have such a strong bond like mother and daughter. Every Tuesday, baby Rebecca spent the day with Valerie. With Valerie's unannounced evening visits and as she would settle in on the sofa, her first question changed from being 'is the kettle on?' to 'can I give the wean her bath?' wean is a Scottish word for little one. Sarah and I would be the helpers, watching Valerie and Rebecca having a great time and listening to Valerie singing old traditional songs for both Sarah and baby Rebecca. Valerie, in the years to come, would refer to herself as Rebecca's other mammy. Who is to argue? I had yet to come across a baby who smiled all the time as Rebecca did. Her beautiful chubby face with beautiful smiles, gifting smiles freely to everybody, and everywhere she was; smiles that would melt any heart.

One spring day, I took Sarah and Rebecca to the local swing park. Disney's movies were getting produced so frequently. When Rebecca was three years old, Disney's "The Aristocats" was out. There is a scene where Thomas O'Malley, the alley cat, climbs up a cherry blossom tree while his girlfriend cat, Duchess, was standing under the tree. Thomas started shaking the branches and showered Duchess with pink petals. As it happened on that day at the swing park, Rebecca was standing and looking adorable under this huge cherry tree which was totally covered with beautiful pink blossom. A young man in his twenties climbed the tree above Rebecca and started shaking the branch and created an identical scene. Rebecca had loved the movie *The Aristocats*, and she loved the movie even more after being showered with pink petals like Duchess.

I gave Rebecca many names yumcious, grumcious, gorgeous, delicious, precious, and later on, having watched children's cartoon Rugrats, I added the name prettyful to the list. We both heard this new word while watching an episode of Rugrats, so I added it to her list of names. Sarah was over six years old when Rebecca was born. As I used to take Sarah to her bed every night, after Rebecca's birth, the three of us went to bed together in Rebecca's room. I had put two single beds next to each other, so the two of them slept next to each other.

Second Encounter

Rebecca was invited to a birthday party of one of her classmates. Rebecca and many of her friends made their way to the birthday girl's house after school. The car Ray and I shared did not have a sat nav, of course, but we did have a little A5 booklet of street maps. I always checked where I was going before I drove off, even in the present time, having sat nav installed in my car. I would also use a highlighter pen on the pages to make the roads I needed to follow stand out. It would make it easier to figure out where I was going. I was to pick Rebecca at 9:00 pm, and the house was on the south side of the city.

After many years of driving, I came to a conclusion which is I should avoid, at any cost, driving during night-time. I hate it. Everything looks different. I can't make out where the curb of the pavements are. The familiar buildings and streets would look nothing like what they would during daytime. I hate it when people wear dark jackets and cross the road whenever and wherever they want. I hate buses. I hate cyclists even more. They are a pain in the neck. We don't have dedicated lanes for cyclists. The Local Council thinks they are being echo friendly for creating cycle paths by narrowing down the car lane. Otherwise, the cyclist would occupy a whole lane. The car drivers would have to patiently wait for a safe opportunity to overtake them. The cyclists didn't abide by any speed restrictions, and they didn't pay road tax. And it was our responsibility to avoid them. Those who annoy me most were the ones who would be speeding, disregarding a twenty-mile zone road. Also, if there were two of them, then they would be competing with each other and at times cycling alongside each other rather than behind each other.

However, most of all, I hate driving to a place I have never been before at night-time. I had the little book of street maps next to me on the passenger seat. I lost count of how many times I had to stop to find out where I was at and more, importantly, was I following the route on my street maps. Because the street maps booklet was an A5 size sheet so to follow any route, you would be flipping different pages in order to get to the end of the route. For example, if you were at page 17 and the road you are on continued, then there would be a note on the right-hand side of page 17 to say go to page 31 (for example) for the continuation of this road. If this road happened to appear at the bottom of page 17, then there would be a note to tell you to go to page 53 (for example) to follow the continuation of this road, and so on. If you had never used these kinds of books, then lucky you. I guess there would've been many heated arguments between partners, one driving the car and the other one looking for direction using this stupid booklet. Although I struggled with my predicament, I was still lucky Ray wasn't with me in the car. In situations like this, one would've resulted in one of us leaving the car after having a loud shouting, 'I am not listening to you' session.

What makes things worse, of course, roads have names, not numbers. I forgot to say I hate city planners too. Why were they allowed to plan the streets so narrow and the areas so dense? So, I got to a place and stopped the car as I knew I was going around in circles. I checked my booklet again. At times I had to reverse the car a bit in order to read the name of the street. Usually, the name of the street is placed high up on the wall of a house at the end of the terrace or written on a plaque erected less than a metre in height at the end of a street. I gave myself plenty of time, knowing how amazing my sense of direction was. So, I was lost. This fact made my mind get all fuzzy and tense. I would hate to be late for Rebecca, and I was really trying my best to focus, but it wasn't happening. I had no idea where I was. I lost count of how many times I stopped and checked the map. So not paying much attention to what was going around me; apparently, I had stopped the car on the zig-zag area before the pedestrian's traffic lights. I was so intently looking into this map when I noticed two men approaching me. They were men in uniform; more precisely, I was caught by the police. I rolled my window down, and before they said anything, I muttered: 'I am so sorry. I really don't know where I am. I have been going around and around in circles.'

They asked: 'Where do you want to go?' So I gave them the address. I was sure they would give me the direction, so I was like a pupil in a classroom trying to memorise what they were saying. Turn right then turn left then blah blah blah. I did follow their directions, though and I did manage at the end to get to the stupid address. I went running to the door as if this one minute would make any difference to how late I was. The party was over, and every other guest had gone home. Rebecca was the last one to be picked up. I apologised profusely.

The lady who opened the door was very kind. She said: 'Don't worry, lots of people get lost when they come to our house.' Once inside the car, I explained to Rebecca why I was late.

She said, 'It is okay, Mum.' She must've noticed how flustered I was. As I switched the car engine on how I wished I didn't need to, and instead we had arrived home. It was nearly ten o'clock. It had passed my bedtime. Now I had to go through that agony all over again. What was worse, I had precious cargo in the car this time around. I had to say so many silent prayers and so quickly.

So, I drove around the area again. I was lost so many times, even in the dark, I could tell I had already been in that spot before. I stopped the car to check the map. I was not sure what was going on, but Rebecca and I saw men, big men, with long bats holding them as if they were their weapons. More men were coming out from this house where I had parked the car. These men were shouting and pointing to the house they came out from so aggressively. I quickly drove off with no hesitation, even though I didn't know where I was going. I was now so angry with myself but at the same time feeling so sorry for myself. My face started feeling numb. I kept rubbing my face as if I was trying to bring it back to life. Of course, I tried my best to keep this to myself, so Rebecca does not get upset. Suddenly, I saw the lights of a car facing me. I had no idea what was going on, so I stopped the car. The next thing I saw was the same two policemen coming towards me. I said to myself, tearing up: 'What have I done now this time?'

I rolled my window down, again, and this time I was like no words, just watery eyes. My tears spoke for me. We had already met. They knew I was to pick my child up, and I was still here, not at home. They said to me: 'Do you realise that you are driving in the wrong direction of the road?'

I apologised again, and said: 'I really don't know where I am and how to get out of here.'

They said to me calmly, 'Take five minutes. We will stop the traffic.' They gave me the directions, this time for how to get home. I took a deep breath. I started the car again with no energy left in me. This time Rebecca was listening to the instructions the policemen gave. She repeated them to me at each corner or turn of the road. Soon we were in familiar surroundings. I took charge this time. We got home with no penalties. I was very grateful as each time I had an encounter with the policemen; they were angels wearing police uniforms.

The area, next to where we lived in Moulin Terrace, was famous for knife crime and drug dealing. It was here, where for the first time, I met a young lady who was in her twenties with a scar across her face from her mouth to her ear. The shameful aftermath of slashing someone's face with a knife was such a callous and evil act. All for drugs and caused by drug dealing.

Sarah was in her last year at primary school. The Local Council was planning to build a brand-new secondary school on the other side of our house. A small green area separated my neighbourhood from where the new school grounds would be. This school was to host pupils from two other schools; their buildings were getting demolished. One of the two schools was situated in a rough area where the crime was a daily occurrence. I did not want Sarah to attend the new school, but she had to as we lived in the catchment area of this new school. Sarah was too precious and too innocent to be surrounded by the life of drugs and crime. So, I took my worries to my God. I talked to Ray about it too, and it caused him to get worried too. We decided it was time we moved to another area with a better school.

I started looking for a new home in the Ralston area in Paisley. As I didn't know the area very well, I would drive through the local streets in the evenings and watch for any sale signs. We went to view a few houses, none of which was suitable. One evening I was driving through Lanfine road from the end where it meets Hawkhead road. As you drive up the road, you would notice the road becomes hilly gradually. The houses on each side of the road looked so beautiful. I didn't say a word but kept driving slowly. What enhanced the scenery, even more, was the beautiful sun facing me as I was driving up the road. I didn't even dare ask my heavenly Father for a house in this street. Houses on this road would've been way over our budget. I kept my lips tight, but my heart was doing the talking with my Father above. Only He knew my heart's desire. There were no sale signs on Lanfine Road. I went back home, having added a bit more to my knowledge of the area. Our budget was £80,000 considering the salaries of both Ray and me; this would've been the upper limit of what the bank would offer us as a loan. A few days later, Ray said to me: 'There is a house for sale in Lanfine road.'

I said to him: 'I don't think so. I drove through this road a few days ago. The houses are beautiful, and I am sure they are very pricey. Plus, I didn't see any sale signs up.' He took the address from the newspaper, and we drove through Lanfine road. We got to the house, and there was no sale sign up. We thought since we were at the doorstep, there was no harm in checking so, we rang the doorbell.

The house belonged to Mr and Mrs Stewart. An elderly couple, who didn't want to attract any attention. So, they chose not to have the sale sign up. The house had been in the market for months, but it didn't attract any buyers. Although the house looked superb in terms of its design, you just have to ignore the cosmetics from the outside, the inside. The carpet was like a hundred years old, and the wallpaper was the same age. The first thing which grabbed my attention was the stunning daylight that came through the stained-glass window on the sidewall next to the stairs. The stairs were wide at the bottom and narrowed a bit as you went up. I could see Sarah, who was still twelve years old, with her wedding gown climbing down these stairs. If you ignore the paintwork and the content of the rooms, the design of every room was beautiful. Each, with its own character. If I didn't pay attention to cosmetics then Ray was even better. He noticed areas, width, length, height, daylight, whether it is south facing, etc. etc. So, as we viewed the various parts of the house, Ray was ticking lots of boxes in his head, and so was I. We wanted the house. Mr Stewart, without making it too obvious, was desperate to sell the house. He wanted £80,000 for the house, not one penny less. He got it, and we got the house. I looked up to heaven with gratitude. It was then when I believed my God does not only hear my spoken prayers, but

He answers the unspoken prayers too. I didn't even dare to dream to live in Lanfine Road, but with my God, life and dreams could happen. My God was preparing my house in Lanfine Road for me. He removed the desire to buy this house by other potential buyers and prepared Mr Stewart's thoughts to ask for the price we could afford.

I loved the house. We gradually managed to update bits and pieces. In time we ended up having the bathroom and the kitchen tile. Rebecca and Sarah shared the big room and the smaller room. Rebecca was like Sarah's shadow. One minute the two of them would be in one room, and the next minute they both would move to their other room. The back garden was filled with mature bushes and amazing flowers. They would be in full bloom at various times in the year. It was in Lanfine I came to learn about bluebells for the first time. We had them growing in the back garden around March time. Rebecca discovered them first. She was only three years old. She would go to the back garden and pick a bunch of bluebells and give them to me. I loved them in her little hands. They looked beautiful, and they smelled beautiful like my three-year-old Rebecca. Rebecca holding a bunch of bluebells is a masterpiece picture no artist could ever replicate. We had a great time me and Rebecca in Lanfine. Every time new flowers blossomed, sure, Rebecca would pick some and give them to me. I loved her precious gifts, and I think Rebecca loved giving them to me. At least three times, she was stung by wasps or bees while picking these flowers, and yet it did not stop her from picking flowers for me. She was too good to be referred to as "a human being". Every year since I would get bluebells from Rebecca the minute she spotted them. When she got older, I would pick them for her instead.

Rebecca developed hay fever when she was twelve years old, so instead of taking the bluebells to her room, I would place them in a vase on the dining table or on the piano in the hallway, so she could see them. Every year she noticed them with a smile.

Years later, Rebecca would mention to her dad and me that she really liked to have a tattoo, but she wasn't sure what. It was her way of getting our approval. Her dad dismissed the idea. He wouldn't agree to stain her body with any tattoos. I suggested words in Aramaic since her dad can write the language. I can only speak it. Rebecca wasn't sure about what I had suggested but was too polite to say no thank you. Since she likes Bob Dylan's music, she said, 'I might pick one of his lyrics.' I didn't comment as I would've liked it if it was Scripture. So, one evening, Rebecca didn't come to the dining table; instead, she stayed in her room as she had dinner with her friend. She had turned twenty-one years old recently. I went to her room as I usually do to ask how her day was. I was totally gobsmacked. So, there were feelings, and there was this one. I was not sure how and what to feel. She had a big smile on her face, and she said, 'I had a tattoo done today,' and she paused, so did I. Both smiling and intensely looking at each other's eyes. As I couldn't see any tattoos on her face or on her neck, I kind of felt relieved. So, I said, 'What is it?' followed by an even more impatient question, 'Where is it?' So, she pulled her top up, slowly and carefully not to touch the painting, and there it was. It was huge both in size and meaning. It was beyond what my mind could take in. Rebecca had this beautiful bluebell tattoo on the side of her torso, starting from under her armpit and down all the way to her waist. It was the size of my hand, so delicately crafted. It was a piece of art. I didn't know what to say. She was watching me with intense, holding her breath, waiting for my reaction. What could I say? How could you describe this? My brain tried and failed to come up with words to describe how I felt about it. I was too charged with emotions, so I said, 'Wow, bluebells, I am really and deeply touched,' and I continued, 'You have no idea how much this means to me.' We cuddled for a long while, longer than usual. I was mindful not to hurt her or touch her side as it was still painful. So, I started asking motherly questions, 'Is it sore?' She took charge of the conversation next and told me all about it and the cleansing solution she was given. Since then, and from time to time, I would ask her to lift her top to let me see the bluebells tattoo resting there in its hiding place. It pleased me to think bluebells meant as much for Rebecca too.

Chapter 15

The Red Robe

When my brother-in-law completed his PhD; for me, it was an example of when life was being just. He was a very clever man, and he worked so tirelessly as a research assistant, but he never received any recognition for his hard work. Although he was not my son – in fact, he is a few years older than me – I felt like a proud mother. Proud of what he finally managed to win what he truly deserved. Since his arrival and being part of our little family in Oxford, I did take care of him as a mother would. He was the only family member living with us away from home. We treasured having him as part of our little family unit. No wonder Sarah once asked me when she was three years old, 'Is it okay to love Uncle as much as I love Dad?' She grew up with him being around. He shared her childhood and loved her as if she was his own daughter. So, when it was time for the graduation ceremony, I bought myself a very beautiful navy-blue midi dress with nice thin material but lined. It had lots of little white buttons at the front and all the way down. The sleeves were short and very smartly made, and the skirt was flowy. It was the best. My favourite dress I have ever put on. It wasn't expensive, but it looked expensive, which for once I didn't mind. Sarah was four years old. I bought her a beautiful pink dress with flowers. It had a little short pale pink cardigan to match but what Sarah loved most was the little bag which came with it. I felt Ray, Sarah, and I were representing all of Ray's family, and so it was even a bigger day for me. First thing in the morning, while getting ready, Ray and his brother were transported to their childhood environment. I enjoyed listening to them, laughing and remembering their mischiefs and the tricks they got up to, annoying their siblings and other relatives, describing in detail their dad and grandpa's reactions. It was like a competition who would remember the next story first. They even used a hairdryer for the first time. Mind you, the room was suffocating with two young men's cologne filling the air. We got to where the ceremony hall was with plenty of time. We met and greeted many people from his work. Then, the proudest moment arrived.

I was on the edge of my seat when it was his turn to be presented with his certificate. The lady who was introducing the next student would be saying a word or two about each one of them. But when it was my brother-in-law's turn, it wasn't a word or two; she said a lot of words. Big words. Probably words she had never said before about any other student graduating that year. She shared with the audience the fact my brother in law's PhD project was the first project ever that brought the most funds to the university in its all history. I jumped on my feet, clapping so hard, my hands were sore. I felt like saying could we rewind in case some people didn't quite hear the wow statements. While clapping, I was exploding with emotions. He made it. He finally made it. It wasn't his dream only, but it was Ray's dream, his parent's dream and everybody else's who knew him and longed for this day to happen. I was the only person who was clapping, but because I clapped so hard, it was like as if the whole audience was clapping. Other people joined in after. After the graduation ceremony, we were invited by his supervisor for a nice meal, and the celebration continued throughout the day. And throughout the whole day, one person was on my mind, his mother, Miriam.

I thought of Miriam and how she would've wished to be here. She would've made even more effort to look her best and stand out from the crowd. Who would've blamed her? Her second son was getting a PhD degree, the highest qualification in his field. So, I decided to record on paper every moment of the day from when we first woke up till we went to bed on that glorious day. It was a very long letter, and I posted it to Miriam. I said to myself, 'If Miriam can't be here today, then I will take the day to her.' I also posted some photos from the day. Years later, when Miriam had left home and joined us. One day she reminded me of the precious letter she received about her son's graduation. I had totally forgotten all about it.

She cuddled me for a long time, saying, 'The letter was the best gift anyone could've given her.' My mother-in-law does not show affection as much. Being a mother of five boys and the headteacher of a big school didn't help. And so, when you get a cuddle from her, you had to accept it as a very special moment. Apparently, when she read the letter, she cried and cried like never before. During this time, my father-in-law came into the house and called for her, but he didn't get any reply. He found her in her bedroom, sitting on her bed. One look at her and his heart sank. He was terrified, thinking the worst had happened. She said to me, describing that moment: 'I couldn't even speak. The words couldn't come out easily to tell him what was going on. So, I gave him the letter to read.' They were both touched by the effort I made to let them enjoy what was rightfully theirs, but life was cruel enough to deny them to be present on a special day like that. After his graduation, my brother-in-law stayed working at the university, utilising the amazing techniques he adopted in his field. The business started pouring from all around the world. What started as his PhD project, with him and his supervisor, ended up being a company employing twenty-nine people. Soon, money was easy and flowing. This time, Ray and I were in someone's mind.

My brother-in-law had achieved his academic goal. It was followed by financial riches. Shortly after, my brother-in-law came to visit us. He said to me, 'Please do me a favour, and go and find any house you like. I will gladly pay for it. I am giving you a blank cheque. Don't think about the cost. Just do me a favour, please, and find a nice big house, any house you want.'

What God did through my brother-in-law was like, for every penny, we send home to help the family members to flee for their lives, we were rewarded with countless pennies and much more. I could humbly say that one fact I know about myself is that I couldn't accept gifts easily. I felt so uncomfortable receiving a gift. The minute I received it, my mind started planning as to how to repay the giver of this gift, with what and when. This time was different, though. I never felt guilty about receiving this amazing gift because I knew the source of it. It came from my Father above. My brother-in-law had so much money that his gift for us didn't affect his bank balance much. I got overwhelmed with emotions and gratitude when my God showered me with His goodness. I looked up, my eyes welling up with burning tears. 'Who am I, Lord? And why do you love me so much?'

Since we liked the area we were living in, so we didn't want to move away to a different one. We started looking for a detached house. After a short period of time, the house with the name Woodend came up for sale. It was a bungalow with two bay windows at the front. It had four bedrooms and three public rooms. The kitchen was in the back. The dining room had stairs, which took you downstairs to a huge public room. This downstairs room had a French sliding door at the far end, which opened up to the back garden. The first time I saw the downstairs room, I thought of it being used as a prayer room, which we did once we moved into the house. The house belonged to the Bryce family. The grandfather had built the house in the early 1930s. Mr and Mrs Bryce had died. Their son and daughter wanted to sell the house, so each could get their share of the inheritance and, in turn, buy their own property. When Ray and I went to view the house, the estate agent had organised an open day for viewing. All potential buyers were invited. There were so many interested parties. Every room I went to see was filled with lots of people. The whole place was so crowded.

We took our time viewing the house. As I kept going from one room to another, my mind took me back to when I was fourteen years old. My whole family was lodging in a two bedroomed house with one public room. My family occupied one of the two bedrooms. We must have spent most of the time outdoors and only entered our sardine-packed space to sleep. The landlord was a distant relative who very kindly agreed to attach us to his own family. My bed (mattress) was on the floor next to my mum's. My youngest sister on my other side. My two brothers had a bed each, and my older sister used the couch as her bed. My older sister was a third-year university student. My brother was preparing for his baccalaureate exam, and I was studying for my national exam, which we had to sit while at middle school. This was one of the three rented accommodation we lived in before my parents built their own house. Buying or renting a house in those days was a rare occasion. We never complained or felt any less than anybody else; on the contrary, we were a very happy family. After all these years to end up having Woodend as my house has left me forever grateful.

Woodend house was neglected, to say the least. None of its renovation needs registered with Ray. He saw space, and he liked it. The front garden was spacious with beautiful established roses and various plants I was yet to learn their names. Unlike any other house I had lived in, this one had two front gates. The wider gate, the start of the driveway, led to a nicely designed old fashioned square-shaped garage at the back of the house. The back garden was huge. For many people, the road – where Woodend house was situated – was a dream place to live. But for us, it was more than that. It was a gift, and therefore it will always be a very special place since and till my dying days. The house went to a closing date as many potential buyers placed an offer. Usually, the house would go to the highest bidder but paying cash would be an influental factor. Ray was encouraged to place an offer to warrant he was the highest bidder. Our offer was the highest and in cash, so the house was ours. We were over the moon, knowing well enough we really didn't deserve it, yet Ray was holding the keys. A song came to mind which I used to sing to Sarah when she needed some encouragement. 'He who began a good work in you, will be faithful to complete it. He who started the work will be faithful to complete it in you.' And so it was with Woodend.

The house was renovated from top to bottom, totally gutted. It was all re-plastered. An electrician and his team were hired to rewire the whole house. A plumber and his team replaced all the radiators, the pipes and the boiler. The flooring was fixed. The downstairs room needed an extra bathroom. A brand-new kitchen and two bathrooms were fitted. The house was wallpapered and painted inside and out. All the gutters were replaced. The girls each picked her room, their furniture and the wallpaper to match. Woodend was rebirthed. Every time I came to visit the house to check on the progress taking place, tradesmen working tirelessly with great craftsmanship, workers' faces were transformed into my Father's angels delivering gifts at their best.

When all the building and the renovating work was completed, the empty rooms needed to be filled with furniture. And yes, my brother-in-law paid for the furniture and the light fittings for each room. During his annual leave, he spent the two weeks with my husband fitting the bedrooms and dining room furniture with joy-filled with pride. Ray was supposed to help, but, honestly, most of the work was done by my brother-in-law. For the most part, Ray's job was to give instructions. With every job completed and as I thanked my brother-in-law, every time his answer was 'bassita', which means 'this is easy'. Bassita was followed with a familiar phrase of his, 'koll youm hitchi waket', which translates to 'every day this time'. It was such an endearing way of his to say, 'With my pleasure.' I do believe he was so proud to be able to provide for his brother in one in a lifetime chance. So, when it was time to move to Woodend, we didn't bring anything from Lanfine. We walked into a brand-new house with everything in it brand new and two new cars in the driveway.

Both Sarah and Rebecca had a friend called Jenny. At times, and while chatting, it was hard to know which Jenny we were referring to. We ended up saying their surname to distinguish one from the other. When Sarah was nearly ten years old, Jenny's mum suggested, 'How about if you and I take Sarah and Jenny for a visit to London? We can take them to the theatre to see Lion King?' Sarah and Jenny screamed with joy. So, we agreed on a weekend which suited all of us. It was Sarah's first-time visiting London. Since Jenny's mum was to take care of organising every detail, who was I to say no. I only had to arrange a sleepover for Rebecca at her friend Jenny. Rebecca was just as excited, even though it was yet another sleepover. Jenny's mum, another friend of mine, was very fond of Rebecca. So, it was agreed Rebecca was going to stay with her Jenny, while Sarah and I would fly away to explore London with Jenny and her mum. As for Ray, he was happy to be left alone, fending for himself for one weekend.

Although I had been to London before, all the visits were for a specific purpose; so it was in and out of the city, never to explore. Jenny's dad used to fly to London frequently to meet his clients. As it happened, he was staying in London during our visit. Jenny's mum drove us to the airport, which was probably a forty minutes' journey. We left the car in the airport car park. Jenny's mum suggested we buy the tickets for London city bus tours at the airport as they were much cheaper than buying them in London. Jenny's mum must've made this journey many times as she seemed to know exactly where to go and what to do. I, however, was happy to follow her lead, being almost like the third kid. Jenny's mum explained the options we had and the places we could visit. Whatever Sarah and Jenny suggested, I was happy to agree to. I loved watching Sarah's face fill with excitement as we hopped from one place to another. The tickets we bought at the airport included a free pass to a boat trip on the River Thames. It was amazing, a great history lesson, and worth every penny. A visit to Oxford Street was a must as Jenny's mum loved shopping. The girls loved being inside Hamley's children big store, taking their time exploring every department. It was such an eventful day. In the evening, we met Jenny's dad before we were off to enjoy the Lion King, another amazing experience. It was all good so far.

The following day was just as good, more shopping, more exploring. As the queues for Madame Tussauds were too long and to the disappointment of the girls, we ended up changing plan, and we ended up hopping on the city tour bus. However, soon I developed a problem. My head was so itchy. I couldn't think of it being so itchy before. Jenny's mum said, 'Maybe it is the shampoo at the hotel that is causing it.' Since I had no other explanation, I agreed. We had another great day, and at some point, we stopped by Boots the Chemist as I bought a bottle of Elvive shampoo, the one we used at home. I had to, especially when Sarah started scratching her head too.

Both Sarah and I loved London, and although there was so much to see, I thought the two nights were enough. I was missing Rebecca like mad. The shampoo I bought didn't make any difference. We arrived home in time to enjoy Rebecca. The scratching continued the next day. I went to the shops and bought a tea tree oil, thinking we had suddenly developed sensitive skin, both Sarah and I at the same time. Was it the washing powder the hotel used to clean the pillowcases? I had to discard this suggestion as Rebecca started itching her head too. Sarah said, 'Mum, do you think it might be nits?' I had to pause for a while to remind myself of this strange and unexpected piece of information I heard.

I replied with total shock and disbelief. I said, 'You mean nits? Creepy crawlies in my hair?' I didn't wait for her to reply. I didn't know what to do, but like an idiot I screamed with disgust, shaking my hands and jumping up and down screaming 'NOOOOO!' The thought of things freely moving around my hair, sucking my blood whenever they wanted, made me feel sick. If possible, my thoughts were, *can I get a new head, one free of nits?* Nits in three locations inside the house, Sarah's head, Rebecca's head and my head, yuk. Perhaps, and by now, there was an army worth of horrible creatures in our heads. Up until that day, I never had nits before, and I honestly had no idea what to do. Yes, I remembered then, and as it happened, and from time to time, more accurately once a year, I would find a letter from my girls' school informing the parents about an outbreak at school. The topic in those letters, of course, never concerned me. So, the letters always ended up in the bin. I had to collect my thoughts and act quickly. I took the girls to the front room and shut the door behind us. I was too embarrassed. Why? I don't know. I didn't want my husband or, even worse, his family to know. These creatures had to go.

I checked on the internet what to expect while Sarah and Rebecca were getting all excited as if we are having this mysterious once in a lifetime experience. Probably they

163

couldn't wait to tell their friends. Heads had to be checked, so we started with Rebecca. The three of us sat on the carpet with the coffee table in front of us. The plan was to spot this ugly thing, and if so, then we are all hit. Sarah's head was right next to mine, slowly leaning forward and staring intently at Rebecca's head. We held our breaths. Rebecca was bending her head so uncomfortably. I hoped so much Sarah was wrong. Yet, our search became almost like a competition between Sarah and me. Who was going to find the first louse? Sarah was right as we found one. I hated being me at that moment. Being a mother, it was my duty to pull the louse out from the long strand of Rebecca's beautiful long hair. I had to do it. I didn't close my eyes as I would've preferred to have done. I narrowed down where the thing was, and I pulled it, moving it all the way to the end of the hair. Being such a tiny beast, it hardly registered whether I had caught something. I rubbed the tips of my fingers together to shake it off and drop it on the coffee table. The three of us stayed a bit back from the coffee table, staring at the thing from afar. Without conferring, we then leant forward, closer to the coffee table to inspect and confirm if this thing was a louse. I am not sure if the louse moved or was it our imagination; we jumped back and away from the table screaming. All the three of us at the same time falling on our bottom. Now, although it was the tiniest creature ever, it felt like it was a dinosaur. This thing had to be killed, and I did it by pressing hard the back of a pen on it, yuk yuk. I continued searching for more, and I got eighteen of them out of Rebecca's hair only. I slaughtered them all. There were less in Sarah's hair. I drove to the chemist to get a special shampoo. I was back in no time. I whispered to the lady at the counter, thinking the whole world was listening. I was advised to buy a certain metal comb as well, which of course I did. I bought too many bottles, far more than what I needed. The fighting spirit of a mother stirred inside me. So, with full determination, I promised myself I wouldn't be sleeping the night unless I had all the beasties killed.

I cut my girls' hair and mine, short and neat. The girls and I had yet another shower, using the special shampoo this time. With the newly bought comb, countless lice were caught. All the bedsheets were binned, the house cleaned and the battle, I think, was won. Months later, the three of us were still traumatised by the experience. We were always watching out for any signs of a revisit. We became suspected the source was Rebecca's Jenny as unfortunately, Rebecca endured another episode after a sleepover at Jenny, so we thought.

Chapter 16

Snowdrops

When I was a teenager, I had the mind of a little girl. Perhaps I had a happy childhood, so the inner me didn't want to grow up. Even as a middle-aged and greyed hair woman, at times, I forget my age and immersed myself in a childlike act or attitude. Little things cheer me up like balloons floating freely on the carpet or spraying water on one of my girls and run for my life, expecting her to chase after me. I learnt not to do this to Ray as the reaction I got from him was not pleasant. He missed the fun as usual. I could relate to little girls' minds. I understood their language. I went down to their level and had more fun than being my age. Grownups make things more complicated than they need to be. We lose the purity and the innocence once we used to have when we were children. I believed God knew my heart's desire and gave me three wonderful girls. I loved talking with them, telling them stories, and listening to their stories. I would invent games to play, on the spot at a time, which we would enjoy playing for hours. I enjoyed their lives, their way of thinking and everything about them. My girls liked my company, and I liked theirs. I didn't think for one moment girls are better than boys, but I know I would have struggled if I had to raise up boys rather than girls. Once I watched a little boy, three years old, when he didn't have anything to kick, he started kicking the wall. Why? Who knows?

I wasn't even twenty years old when, one day, my God spoke to me through a vision. I was at university, and it was in the afternoon. As I did an engineering course, the campus was full of young men. In those days, there weren't many female students who would choose to do an engineering course. Being an adult educational establishment, you don't get visitors with children, so the chance of seeing a little girl in the vicinity was very remote. The campus had many buildings. One day, I was walking towards one of the buildings to attend a chemistry lab. On the left-hand side of the footpath was the civil engineering building, and on the right-hand side was an open space. Much further to the right was another building where the chemistry lab was situated. I looked up to the right, about ten metres away from me, and I saw a little girl on her own. She was probably four years old with dark brown hair and a fringe. I can't remember any details of what she was wearing, but she had a little dress on with a sash tied to the back. The dress had two little pockets at the front. I can't remember the colour of her dress, but it was pale colours. As I have always loved little girls, I looked with a smile on my face. And for a fraction of a second, I must've blinked or looked ahead then looked back towards the little girl, but she wasn't there. I never thought anything of this. But many years later, when my Rachel was four years old, one day I was looking at her, and I said to myself, 'I have seen Rachel before.' I instantly remembered the little girl God showed me many years ago before even I was engaged to her dad. Although by now, I had Sarah and Rebecca, the little girl

I saw in a vision somehow came alive only when I was looking at Rachel that day. Rachel was a gift from God, a very special one. It fills my heart and my life with a feeling of warmth and joy just to know she is mine.

While I was pregnant with Rachel, I had a prenatal clinic on a Friday at 2:00 pm at what used to be called Southern General Hospital in the city. Nowadays, it is a huge complex, probably the biggest in Europe, and the name has changed to Queen Elizabeth Teaching Hospital. Ray drove me to the hospital for my appointment. I saw the nurse first. I had my urine tested. I was then asked to wait to be seen by the midwife. Once I was examined, I was told I had to stay the night in the hospital since the baby would be coming out soon. I had dilated two centimetres already. Rachel was born at 4:40 pm on that special day, so beautiful and healthy. At the start of my pregnancy, and since I was 38 years old, I was offered to have an ultrasound test done to find out if my baby was going to have a down syndrome. I, of course, declined the offer. Apparently, every pregnant woman would be offered to have the test done if she was over 34 years old. Apart from a good appetite and morning sickness, everything else during my pregnancy was fine. I was delighted with everything had gone well, both baby and mother. Rachel was perfect. Once Ray spent some time with baby Rachel, I asked him to go home, pick Rebecca up from nursery. He then had to go and pick Sarah up from after school care. He had to feed them both, get them ready and drive them to the hospital to meet their new baby sister. The visiting hour was from 7:00 pm. Having had two babies already, I was counted as an experienced mother, so I wasn't given much attention in the hospital ward. I had the hospital dinner then I got myself and the baby ready to greet her big sisters. A few minutes after 7:00 pm, Valerie came to visit Rachel and me. She had beautiful flowers and a nice card for Rachel. I was so pleased to see her, my Valerie, always close to me. Valerie held Rachel in her arms and couldn't stop complimenting her. I watched the two of them and smiled. There was no sign of Ray and the girls. Valerie and I both wondered where Ray was and why is it taking him so long to come. We talked for a while, thinking Ray and the girls would appear any minute. Valerie had to leave soon to give Sarah and Rebecca the chance to hold and meet their baby sister. Still no sign of Ray and the girls. As I didn't have a mobile phone, I had to go and use the phone in the ward. Having gone through giving birth a few hours earlier, I couldn't walk at a fast pace. Before I even reached where the nurses congregate, I had to change the plan and visit the bathroom first to clean myself. I know I had issues with bleeding after giving birth, so perhaps I should stay in bed, but how could I when your visitors forgot all about you and the new baby. I finally got hold of a phone and dialled the house number. It kept ringing out; no one picked up. I dialled the number again, still no reply. I hung up, puzzled but managed to wobble back to my bed. I said to Valerie, 'Do you think they are okay?'

'Of course,' she said. She then said, 'You know what men are like. It must've taken him ages to get the girls ready. He should be here any minute.' She continued, 'I better be off. I will come and see you both tomorrow.' It was almost 7:30 when Valerie left. No sign of Ray and the girls. The other three patients had so many visitors, coming and going, and I had only Valerie. She came and went, and since I had been waiting and waiting, no other visitors for me. Every minute passed felt like an hour. It was now 7:45. I started worrying, so I checked on Rachel, who was fast asleep in her little cot next to my bed. I decided to go and see the nurses to let them know my husband was on his way, and he would be bringing my two other daughters to see their newly born baby sister.

I said to them, 'I am not sure why they are not here yet, but I know they must be on their way. Could you please let my family stay a bit longer after the visitation period is over?' Now that this was agreed upon, I went back to my bed and waited.

It was nearing 8:00 pm, and there was still no sign of Ray. I knew something was wrong. Something must've happened; otherwise, Ray would've been here. I started calculating how long he would need to pick two children – one from school, one from the nursery – feed them, got them ready and drive 15 minutes journey to the hospital. Could he do this in less than three hours? All the other visitors had left, and it was all quiet for a while in the ward. I shut the curtain around my bed, took Rachel in my arms and started sobbing, thinking of the worst. Now I was worried sick. I started telling myself they are gone, all the three of them are gone, and it was just me and Rachel left. Every moment felt like a year now. No matter how hard I tried to think positive, I couldn't help imagining Rebecca and Sarah' s faces, screaming with fear and calling for me. It was like you knew you should be out there looking, checking, asking, just doing something. In times like these, I wish there were so many copies of me, sending each one in a different direction like little soldiers, one with wings, one with big long legs, another one with a speed of light, kind of speed going through walls like ghosts. My whole world was reduced to a few hours old baby and me, alone on a hospital bed.

My ears were attentive, waiting to hear Sarah and Rebecca approaching and opening the curtain with excitement and big smiles; instead, a nurse came to see me. She slowly opened the curtains, and then she said in a low voice: 'I am sorry to say, but your husband phoned to say there has been an accident. Your little girl is okay, but your older daughter is hurt.' That was it, no details. Accident? Was Sarah hurt? How and why? What exactly happened? Where were they? What was happening now? I had no answers. Was there another car or cars involved? I knew Ray could be an impatient driver; no, he was an impatient driver all the time. Could he not for once ignore other drivers and be here? I had no idea what to say or what to do. I knew for sure though Ray didn't do well in emergencies. I was the one who took over in situations like this. My physical body failed me in a big way. It kind of felt like a prisoner with chains, being tormented but couldn't react. I never felt so alone, so hopeless and so useless. My Sarah was somewhere hurt, and I was there on a bed, with a few hours old baby. So, who was comforting the three-year-old Rebecca? I couldn't even walk to the bathroom and back without needing to go back again and change my sanitary towels. I was an incompetent wreck.

It was half-past ten before I saw Sarah and Rebecca's lovely faces with their dad. Sarah had a piece of cloth wrapped around her arm, made as a sling to keep her arm up. Apparently, at 6:00 pm, Sarah fell off her bike and hurt her wrist. All this time, the three of them were in the same hospital as mine, but in a different department. I was relieved, of course, but at the same time, unhappy about the timing of this and the lack of explanation given to me. I was shaking with mixed emotions. I didn't think I was fit enough to even talk.

Ray came to see me and to let me know he needs to take Sarah to the Sick Children's Hospital now as she would be operated on first thing tomorrow morning. As a mother, sometimes I felt like an idiot with what I come up with, but that night, I needed three of me. Sarah needed me to take her to the hospital and stay the night with her, comfort her and see to her needs. Yet, it was her dad who stepped up to the task. I was not available when she needed me most. Sarah had never been admitted to the hospital before. Rebecca, up until that morning, was the baby of the family and in some way, the centre of my attention. If I was in the kitchen doing the dishes, Rebecca would be sitting on the floor near my feet, playing with her toys. If it happened, and I needed to go to another room to get something, she would gather her toys very quickly and follow me to the other room. We were together all the time. She did everything with me. We had baths together. I took her to sleep every night. Only recently, she stopped sitting on my knee while eating. Rachel, who was a few hours old, won't even survive without my milk. Rebecca was three years old. She had never gone to sleep on her own. She would have to be away from me all night. Rebecca was looking at me, with a baby in my arms, not her. And, unfortunately, she would need to stay the night at Valerie's. No matter what words I used to explain to Rebecca what needed to happen and the sleeping arrangement for the night, she couldn't understand. She was constantly crying and holding so tightly to my dress. I didn't blame her. She was hurt badly and abandoned by both her parents. I had to phone Valerie and ask her to come to the hospital to take Rebecca with her to stay the night at her house. Valerie arrived within 15 minutes. Sarah and her dad left first. I had a chance to try and comfort

Rebecca and explain to her it was only for a few hours. She would have a sleepover at Valerie's. And when she would wake up, we would have breakfast together. Rebecca continued crying, and so did my heart. All she wanted was her mum. Instead, there was a brand-new baby in her mum's arms, who took her place and stole her mum's attention away from her. Even worse, she had been forsaken and banished to another house. Of course, no matter what Valerie and I said, it made no difference to Rebecca. She was exhausted but could not stop whimpering. Rebecca loved Valerie but not that night. I really hated hospitals that night. Why could not they accommodate a little bed for Rebecca next to mine? I had to walk with Rebecca and Valerie through the hospital corridors as far as I could. Valerie carried Rebecca outside the ward towards the lift. Rebecca's screams became louder with every foot she was getting further away from me. I heard Rebecca's screams way after she was gone. I was left totally broken, shattered emotionally and physically. The only blessing was Rachel being unaware of what was going on the night of her birth. I couldn't wait for the daybreak to discharge myself. Valerie dropped Rebecca off first thing in the morning. What joy? Sarah had her wrist fixed that morning. She came home with a stocky, so I had to look after Sarah and her stocky for the next six weeks, very challenging weeks, to say the least, but we all managed. Soon, we were accustomed to new routines, and life was almost back to normal, except now there were five of us.

Sixteen years later, I dropped Rebecca and Valerie off near the entrance to a concert hall. They were off to be entertained by Bob Dylan, no less. Rebecca had bought two tickets. She said to me, 'I just don't know if he will ever come back to the city again. I will regret it if I don't go. This might be my last chance to see him.' Rebecca and Valerie are both great fans of Bob Dylan. This was Rebecca's first time seeing him live in concert, and it was Valerie's third time. As I dropped them off, they didn't even say bye to me. They were so excited, chatting away. I watched them for a wee while, and I remembered the night Rachel was born, when Rebecca was three years old, screaming in the corridors of the hospital and Valerie carrying her to her house.

Whenever Rebecca would be playing her ukulele or her guitar, singing Bob's songs, the sound of her beautiful voice would draw me to where she was. I would sit and watch her, listening to her beautiful voice. No matter what Rebecca sang, it always felt like heaven, even when I didn't particularly like the tune or the lyric of the song. I always liked to join in once the tune of Bob's song 'Sixteen years' started. Perhaps, this is not the title of the song, who knows. Rebecca would put up with me like I used to put up with my girls when they were wee.

Over two hours later, I was back in the same spot with my car parked, waiting to pick the two of them up. I saw Valerie and Rebecca, and so I waved to them. They did notice me, but they didn't wave back. They were still chatting away, animated with excitement this time. I said, 'How was it?'

The two of them replied at the same time, 'Don't ask.'

Then Rebecca said, 'Let me just enjoy it for now, but I will tell you all about it tomorrow.' Obviously, they did have a great time. I am not sure what do they like about a voice so croaky and angry sounding, and it changes all the time. Of course, I could not express my true opinion about Bob to them. Apparently, the concert was that Bob sat on a chair; just him, with a hat on and a guitar; no smiles; nothing; no chats, he sang then he left.

I said to Rebecca, 'I bet you were the youngest person in the audience.'

She replied, 'I think you are right.'

When we moved to Woodend, Rachel was two years old. I had never seen snowdrops before. Hearing the name, I would not have known what we are referring to. Somewhere, in the front garden, in a small patch near the front gate, tucked under St John's wort bush with its beautiful yellow flowers, lived the snowdrops. Rachel found them first, and she introduced me to them. One February day, Rachel gave me a small bunch of the most stunning and delicate white flowers. Delighted with my beautiful gift, I said, 'Where did you get these exquisite flowers from?' She held my hand, and she took me to the front garden. There were a few of them left as she had picked most of what was there. A few more flowers appeared in the following few weeks. Every year, they would come out in the same spot and with the same numbers. Every year, Rachel would pick the first ones to blossom and give them to me. Years later, when Rachel got older, the roles reversed as I became the one who would pick the snowdrops and give them to Rachel. It was the same story with Rebecca's bluebells. When Rachel stopped bothering about the snowdrops, I continued picking only three snowdrops and leave them on the floor outside her bedroom. A few days later, the three snowdrops would still be there, dry and dead, so I would reluctantly bin them. She would make a point of having noticed them but not interested enough to pick them up. A few years later, the snowdrops and the bluebells would be picked up by me and for me. Life changes things. It changes the meaning of things. Without you realising, you change with it too. Signs of my little ones becoming young ladies. And the young mother becoming an old lady.

Chapter 17

Third Encounter

Sarah moved to live in the north to study for a university course. It had to happen, and we accepted the painful fact with a heavy heart. Rather than walking a few steps to her bedroom to see her, it became over three hours' drive. It took us a long time to get over not having Sarah at home. I didn't know how to cook for four instead of five. There was always left-over food, enough for the fifth person of the family. I would go to her room and pick an item or two of her clothing and add them to the laundry. It was my way of kidding myself that she was still around. Sarah was away for five long years. After five years, she was back home again, where she belonged. Sarah stayed in a flat with a walking distance to the university building. Her dad made sure Sarah's flat was done to her taste. The kitchen had a bright orange wall, a teal wall for the living room, very pale pink for the bathroom and one bright pink wall in her bedroom. As for the front door, it was bright purple.

We didn't give Sarah a chance to pine for us or grow a homesick feeling; instead, we enjoyed her beauty and her presence on a regular basis. There were times when the four of us would make the journey, other times, her dad would go on his own, but mostly, it would be just me. Sarah's one-bedroom flat felt even smaller when all the four of us descended upon her. An eight-year-old Rachel would pick the bathroom and sit on the pink fluffy floor mat and keep herself busy when she needed a break or when she couldn't get the seat that she wanted. At the end of each of our visits, Sarah's flat was left spotless, her laundry done, her meal cooked and her fridge freezer filled with food. One day, and as I was preparing to leave, Sarah said to me, 'You know, Mum, when you are here, it makes me realise how lonely it is without you guys.'

I pretended to answer so causally. 'It won't be for long now. You are here for a reason, and soon you will be back home.' I continued making stories up about how it would be too noisy at home and that she needed her own space, peace and quiet to focus on her studies. I spared her the details of how much we desperately all miss her. Sarah would be in her living room studying, and I would be sitting on the other sofa, minding my own business and soaking up the joy of being close to her.

It was always such a joyous moment when after three hours of driving, I would see the city's lights from a distance. I would have a big smile on my face knowing I was 20 minutes away from seeing my Sarah. On leaving her flat after each visit, and as I turned my car to the right at the end of her street, my eyes would well up instantly. We all knew she was there for a reason. Her dad had a saying: 'Just bring the strawberries and come home.' Meaning, you are here temporarily, and for a purpose: to get your degree.

After one of these visits, and once I had her flat in order, it was time to leave my angel and go home. It was after 9:00

pm. I was about to put my coat on when we looked at each other for a while silently. Sarah said to me in a voice that pierced my heart, 'Mum, please stay just a bit longer.' Of course, I stayed. It was Sunday night, I had a three-hour-long drive ahead of me, and I had work the following morning. Not to mention, I was an early bird, not a night owl. I don't do well staying up late. It was already nearing my bedtime. Never mind these facts, I stayed. Finally, I left. It was just before midnight. I was driving for a long time, and I was probably the only driver on the road. I was sleepy and weary, both physically and emotionally.

The early bird in me kept nagging me for sure. 'I am not going to have enough sleep tonight.'

The many stretches of the motorway didn't have streetlights, so I was driving in pitch-black darkness. I would use the car headlights when there was no incoming traffic to help me see the road better. My body was trying to give up and slide under my seat, but I was fighting the sensation. I felt my eyes slowly close. When I saw signs on the road which said "tiredness can kill", I knew it was true, but there was nothing I could do. I kept rolling the driver's window down to get some fresh air to wake me up umpteen times. If I was brave enough and didn't have work the next morning, I would've pulled over in a parking bay area to nap for half an hour or so, but I couldn't. Each mile was closer to home, to my bed. 'Thirteen minutes to the city.' Great, home soon. It was nearly 3:00 am by now. I kept telling myself I was nearly there and should be able to have at least a few hours' sleep.

Well, I must've dozed off for a moment or two. Within less than a minute, it felt as though I was inside a tiny hobbit room with a very low ceiling. The space around me was in total darkness and silence; I had been transported to another world. My eyes were wide open, stretched beyond their normal size, trying to figure out what was going on. Was it real or a dream? It was real. My twelve-year-old car was spinning out of control at the speed of 70 miles an hour. This was one of the times during which I am convinced God was working overtime for me.

I was aware of my humble strength and less than perfect driving skills, but I also felt with all my being that power beyond mine had taken control. The stretch of the carriageway I was driving on was steep and hilly, with a curve and sharp right, turning to join another part of the motorway. There were huge, wide concrete columns on each side of the road, holding a bridge that joined the motorway. The drop was over twenty metres. If you were to have an accident in that location, it would have been certain death. Most importantly, on the right-hand side, was a very small island. The size of this grassy area was probably ten meters in length and five meters wide. In that moment and in that spot, I believe God showed up in a supernatural way. He pulled my car up with His mighty hand and delivered me safely. The car was now parked in the small grassy area and facing the opposite direction of the traffic. Ray always teased me about how poor my car parking skills are, and I always agreed. However, the manner in which my speeding car ended up perfectly parked on that small island: facing the wrong direction to the traffic, with no damage whatsoever; I bet not even Ray could've parked the car impeccably like that.

My God's rescue plan didn't stop there. When He begins, He faithfully completes the blessing. There was nothing wrong with the car or me. I sat inside the car for a few minutes, mind blank, unable to fully comprehend the magnitude of what had happened. My surroundings were pitch black, and the roads were deserted. I couldn't recall anything, and no one else was involved. Since there was nothing wrong with me, I came to the conclusion that I should go home and leave the contemplation for later.

To my relief, when I started the car, there was a response. Clearly, there was nothing wrong with the engine. I kept thinking: *All I need now is to move the car, turn the steering wheel, join the motorway, and head home.* If only it had been so easy. My car would not budge; I didn't know what was wrong with it. The noise it made when I pushed down on the gas was an abnormal, ominous screech. Assuming that the noise was coming from the wheels, I inspected the car as if I had any idea what to do. The wheels had long, wild grass wound tightly around them, pasted with mud, making it difficult for the wheels to move. The car was stuck. Fused together, the wheels and natural elements became a single entity in that spot. To no avail, I tried with my bare hands to unravel the grass until I heard a man's voice shouting, 'Are you okay?'

I replied, 'Yes, I am, thank you, but the car is not moving.'

He asked what happened and I told him that I didn't know. The man was standing next to his car, parked on the side of the carriageway. He said he was a taxi driver dropping a passenger off when he noticed my car and told me that he had already phoned the police.

Looking up and around, he said, 'I can't see any CCTV cameras here. It could've been a deer or a fox jumped in front of your car.'

Before I knew it, a black and white police car pulled over. Bidding me farewell, the taxi driver drove off. He made me question if I would've stopped to help another human in the same predicament. I wasn't sure.

There were two policemen. The first thing they asked if I was injured.

Nodding, I told them, 'I'm fine, thank you, but my car is stuck.' Thankfully, they never questioned what happened, so I didn't even need to say anything. Unlike me, they knew what to do. They tried to pull my car out, and when it didn't work; they phoned another police car. A 4x4 arrived. Within minutes, they had used thick ropes to pull my car out of the mud. One of the officers put signs on the road in case there was an incoming car. I thanked these night angels, and soon I was back on the motorway. The police car was driving behind me for a while. At some point near the city centre, I looked at my mirror and noticed the police car was not behind me anymore.

The first thing I did when I got home was taking a shower. My body was shaking from inside, and my mind was spinning with unanswered questions: *what if there had been another car on the road? What if my car hadn't stopped? I could've died. Other people could've died.* Did I sleep or faint on the sofa? I woke up after a couple of hours. My body was still in shock. I was up and ready for another day's challenges at work. Not a spot of blood or a fracture, no car repair required, no questioning by the police, no phone calls to the rescue or road assistance; yet again another encounter with my local caring police force. All orchestrated by my Father above.

How can I not boast about His power and protection? I know my redeemer lives. He is all around me, in front of me, covers me like a protective bubble, and inside me, living in every cell in my body. So, there is a lovely hymn which I often sing. 'You ask me how I know He lives? He lives in my heart.' So, when you know God is as real to you like yourself, how can you but live your life as if you have a twin, an invisible twin, so mighty and powerful, living within you, alongside you, yet He has created the universe, and all that is in the sea, in the air, inside every human heart, every detail of every body system, humans to insects, birds, trees all shapes and sizes. This amazing supernatural becomes so natural and chooses to be in my life, wow. Every time I sing the words of a song, *God in Heaven Living in Me*, I have to pause, as my mind gets blown away by this fact, that God in all His majesty is living in me!

Although life is cruel, it has turned my childhood memories into an unreal mirage from an alien world, completely different from mine. When these memories come to mind, my heart relives them, but my world makes them seem distant as if they never happened. My heart was broken, but it was mended by many showers of blessings from above. My God kept His eye on me. Life is never fair; people will always let you down and hurt you. At times, you're so sure that you don't matter to anybody, nobody cares and nobody notices you. But none of these facts matter; what matters is "you and Him, together".

Chapter 18
The Old Lady

Woodend has two front rooms with big bay windows which come down to two feet of the floor. While seated, any person walking passing by my house is clearly visible. One Saturday morning, Ray and I were sipping our coffee in the front room while chatting away. Looking up, the appearance of an old lady grabbed my attention. She would have been in her mid-eighties. She was walking so slowly with the help of a walking stick and face down the whole time. She was wearing a dark grey long raincoat with a hood. Something stirred inside me and caused me to stand up, and watch the old lady intently until she disappeared from my view. The scene filled me with emotions that I couldn't explain, and throughout the day, I couldn't take her out of my mind. Although she was a total stranger, yet my heart was filled with love for her, and I kept wondering who she might be and what kind of life she might've lived. Her house had to be nearby, considering the pace of her walk. It was the following Saturday when I saw her again. This time I stood near the bay window watching her until she went around the curve on the left-hand side of my road. *My mum would've been at a similar age*, I thought. The old lady was perhaps a bit shorter than my mum. Judging by what I saw so far, I presumed she had a nice and gentle nature.

Few weeks prior to spotting this old lady, I had the most amazing and intense encounter. I had travelled to Denmark to visit my two sisters: Barbara and Magdalene. They live near each other in one of the small towns. Although this was my third visit to Denmark yet this visit had very special importance as I met my brother for the first time since I saw him last in 1987 in Oxford. This was thirty years later. My brother and his family live in Australia, now married with three beautiful young ladies whom I had never met. He only stayed in Denmark for three days before he and his family continued their journey touring other European countries. On that special day, my sisters and I went to Copenhagen airport filled with excitement. No words could describe what was going on in my mind. My sisters and I were walking on air like three fluffy, puffy bubbly, too excited fairies. All my emotions were muddled up; I couldn't feel much, I couldn't hear much and I couldn't think much. What was ahead of us was too good to be true. The last time I saw my brother, I was twenty-four years old, and now I was fifty-four years old; the same age as my mum's when I last saw her. Too extreme emotions engulfed me. One minute I was thinking, how can life be so cruel to deny me seeing my brother for thirty long years, and at the same time, I would say how good life was to allow me to see my brother one more time.

We arrived at the airport early. The flight was delayed, so having two older sisters who both were heavy smokers, we were like three lost chickens with no leader. One minute I was annoyed at them for wanting to go out for a cigarette; the next minute, I would change my mind as it gave us something to occupy ourselves with. The excitement made my sisters crave nicotine more than usual. The waiting was cruel. The air inside the airport was not enough to fill my lungs. Anybody in the arrival area watching us would've had a cracking time with fits of laughter at our expense. One minute we were sitting, the next minute, we would stand up and then walk to a different seating area, going out and back to the same spot or not. I lost count as to how many times we checked the arrival screen. Wouldn't it have been good if there were no people around, just us, waiting for my brother and his family?

And before I knew it, I saw him. Every cell in my body froze. I almost had to remind myself to breathe. He had totally shaved his hair, with no moustache, but just as handsome as he was all these years ago. I stood still, wishing I could make the time stand still, too. Glancing to check his wife and his three daughters had safely arrived, I cuddled his wife first and then his three daughters. Totally overwhelmed with emotions. Finally, it was my turn to hold my brother. Being so close to him, I needed someone to tell me what to do next. My brother has a very intense, soulful deep voice; hearing him and seeing him face to face nearly suffocated me.

Although I was close to all my siblings, my brother and I had so much more memories together. We went to the same university and did the same course. He is three years older than me, so we had a very special bond. Because I had left home first, they all knew I had missed him the most. My brother and I held each other for a long while, two middle-aged people filled with emotions and lost for words. We looked like the parents of the same two young people who said goodbye to each other in Oxford thirty years ago. The last time I saw him, he was single and starting to build his future, and on that day, he was exhibiting his future to me in the form of his beloved family. I was full of gratitude to my God for his abundant provision once more.

The following three days were joyous yet at the same time left me feeling deeply defeated, having thirty years' worth of being with him stolen from me. We had a smashing time as every moment was precious. We stayed up late into the early hours, trying to pack in as much closeness and affection for each other as we could. Magical moments like those I dreamt about for so long. To actually live them, having my brother in the same space as I caused my brain wires to go all fuzzy. Even when I was talking to my nieces or my sister-in-law, I would avoid having my back to my brother so I could still see him. He reminded me of so many events that happened in our past that sometimes caused us to laugh and at other times to cry. To my shame, once or twice, I didn't even remember certain events. We would continue chatting, and at some point, we would start singing a song that meant something to all of us. My brother's voice was great to listen to, but he also has a beautiful singing voice. He came prepared as he brought with him a recorder, a proper one, a bought one, not one of those that he used to make, using wild reed plant when we were children. I loved him even more now that he was a full package with a very warm and loving wife and three amazing beautiful young ladies, each of whom would've been any parent's dream come true.

It was time to share gifts. My brother and his family had visited the holy land prior to arriving in Denmark. They spend two weeks during Easter time there visiting all the special and sacred places in a packed program. They shared with us the unique experience and the highlights of their trip. One of the gifts which my brother gave me was a nice rosary which he had rubbed on the tomb of the Lord Jesus in Jerusalem, a very special gift indeed. After my mum had passed away, I had asked if I could have her rosary to keep, the one item which she would've held in her hands the longest period considering how many times a day she prayed. He also gave me a silver pencil and said, 'Ray gave me this mechanical pencil as a gift when we were students at university. I have treasured this gift, and I have kept it all these years. I want you to give it to my friend Ray to let him know how much his friendship means to me.' My brother and Ray would've been in their early twenties when this took place. Would Ray remember it?

All good times come to an end, and so it was with the swift visit of one of the closest people to my heart, my brother. His departure was as emotional as his arrival. My brother's visit had a healing effect on me. For decades I had longed for this opportunity. Year after year, my hope was getting diminished as I almost gave up thinking it could never happen. Yet I did see him, and the doubt was beaten. Seeing my brother again was not an impossibility anymore.

The next time I caught sight of the old lady was after my return from Denmark. I noticed after passing my house she entered a house on top of my road. The house was a nunnery. Nuns lived in that house since we moved into Woodend. So, she must be a nun, a retired nun perhaps, considering her age. Every sense in my body told me I had to go and speak to her. The following Saturday, I saw her again out for her walk. In no time, I got ready, and by the time I left my house, she had gone beyond the curved corner on the left side of my house. With faster steps, I walked in the direction she had gone, trying to catch up with her.

Not wanting to startle her and as I was close to her, I said, 'I am sorry to bother you.' Then I introduced myself, and I said to her and pointed out to where my house was so that she wasn't alarmed by this total stranger who appeared from nowhere. As she was heading home, I asked her if I could walk her home. Gently and slowly, she chatted away; we learnt more about each other and about our faith. She had a very soft and slow voice. She struggled with her eyesight. There was no mention of how I had been watching her as it might have made her feel uncomfortable and perhaps made her question my motive for befriending her, not that anyone looking at me would suggest I was a con woman. 'You remind me of my mother,' I spoke. 'My mother, too, had problems with her sight all her life,' I continued. When I left my house and scuttled after the old lady, my hand was in my pocket the whole time, tightly holding to a very precious gift which I felt belonged to this lady. I said, 'I have a very special gift I want you to have.'

She was taken by surprise, so she said 'A gift? For me?'

I said, 'Yes.' So, I opened my hand and I placed the rosary which my brother gave me and placed it in her hand.

We stopped for a while as if what was taking place commanded its special ceremony. She listened after she asked me to come closer to her good ear. Her eyes were wide open, her head was up now and watching my lips as I told her the story behind the rosary and how precious this rosary was. Then I said, 'Although it means so much to me, I want you to have it.' I continued, 'My brother has been a deacon in a Catholic church since he was eighteen years old. All the prayers he has learnt and said were in Aramaic, the language Jesus spoke.' With emotions so high, I told her about my visit

189

to Denmark and meeting up with my brother, and the rosary was my brother's gift for me. Tears started rolling down her cheeks and mine.

'Nobody has ever given me a present like this.'

So, I said, 'God sees you as His gift, and you are so precious to Him and to me.'

We passed our house, and I pointed out for her where I lived. She could see her house from where we were standing. When we arrived at her house, she invited me in. She was the fittest of the household, but they did have a much younger sister who looked after them all.

One evening, Rachel came with me as we went to see my nun friend. Rachel has a magical way of communicating with people. Rachel's youth and her beautiful smiles brightened their day. We took with us a homemade fruit cake which they were going to have with their afternoon tea. Being indoor and without her dark grey coat on, I could see how frail and weak my nun neighbour looked, but still, she was chatting away, always looking down because of her poor eyesight.

After that visit, I saw my nun friend twice. She wasn't out the following Saturday or the Saturday after that. I didn't want to know why she stopped her walks. I kind of guessed something wrong has happened but I didn't want to know or hear about it, so I never visited her house to ask for her. Selfish, I know, but it was my way of dealing with not seeing her again. I am glad though, I met with her for the few times I did. In my mind, I know I was meant to give her that gift and let her know how special she was. Since then, every time I am in the front room, I would look through the bay window and still vividly see my little old lady's image with her walking stick and her dark grey coat.

Chapter 19

The Crown I Wear

Having my girls and holding them in my arms for the first time were memorable moments that could never fade away. They emit joy unspeakable with every new day. Yet, at times, I felt totally drained as the demand for parenting sucked the life out of me. My time, my thoughts, my energy, my money and everything else belonged to them. Since Sarah was born, I became banished. I wasn't aware children are a huge and lifetime commitment, and they constantly need to be loved, cared for and feel they are wanted.

Raising up my first child, for most of the time, I didn't have a clue what I was supposed to be doing. Sarah and I learnt together how to deal with what life threw at us. Every baby issue I was faced with was happening for the first time. Not having my mother or my extended family nearby didn't help. I had to instantly unravel what Sarah's little adventures and fancies puzzled me with. In those years, God was very close to me, waiting for my next request. I struggled big time, but Sarah was loved and taken care of, even though at times I doubted myself. When she was several months old, she rolled over off my bed and fell on the carpet. I was terrified, thinking she had died despite my bed was a foot above the carpet. It took me a while to get over the shock. Since then, I would always put pillows next to the baby as a barrier and on the floor to fall on. Many years later, the same happened to Rebecca. This time she fell off the sofa. Neither of the two incidents caused any harm to my babies. They didn't even cry. I had fallen off their beds as well, many times, no harm was done either, a bit embarrassed and disoriented for a little while perhaps.

Every night, I would take my girls to sleep. I would tell them stories until they fell asleep. Stories which I made up, of course, or they were my mum's stories. I might have changed them a bit, unintentionally, as at times I would pause, and my mind will go blank. I enjoyed coming up with new stories and imagining conversations and events that pleased my girls. The main characters in my stories had the same names as my girls, whether they were people or little animals. The naming of the characters was suggested by my girls. I would prompt them to guess. 'So what do they think happened next?' It was my way of making them contribute as to how the events of the story would go. However, my creative mind did not serve me well in remembering these details the following night. My little ones would end up correcting me and reminding me how the story went. Rachel would ask for stories from my childhood and the kind of things I got up to. Many of these stories involved my friend Choona. Not often, but at times, I would doze off for a moment or two. They would wake me up and ask me to continue with the story. First, I would be disoriented, thinking to myself, *where am I?*

They would eagerly say, 'What happened next?'

I would quickly gather my thoughts and probe them, 'Where were we?' And so, it continued. If you want to compare my storytelling to my mother's, then she would win.

All the three girls of mine would wake up in the middle of the night, probably until they were five years old. They would call 'Muuuuuuuuuuum.' They only needed to say it once, or so I thought, and I would be up. I would rush to their room with a glass of water and start another story until they fell asleep again. Rachel was probably three years old when this routine was changed forever.

One night, I heard a strange sound in the house. It was of Rachel calling 'Daaaaaad.' I woke up as if I didn't hear it correctly, so she called again 'Daaaaaaaaaaaaaaad.'

I said to myself, 'Dad? Why Dad?' It was like one of the scenes in a Disney movie where Bagheera, a black panther – a fictional character in Rudyard Kipling's Mowgli stories in the Jungle Book – woke up in the middle of the night when it heard the sound of "man-cub" crying, a human sound in the jungle for the first time. I woke Ray up, and I told him, 'Rachel is calling you.' He was as much surprised as I was.

He ran to her bedroom shouting, 'I am coming, I am coming.' I went back to sleep and left him to enjoy the experience of being needed as a storyteller. This was Rachel setting her rules, new rules in the household. Since that night, she would ask her dad to take her to sleep, not me. Not that I minded, but it was strange. He would tell her stories about sharky and barky, the two little shark friends, and the many adventures of detective Mason. Times were changing; especially, when Rebecca would join them and the three of them would go to sleep together. I questioned Ray's choice of topics for his stories, but Rebecca and Rachel insisted on them. Annoyed at being left out and being overlooked despite my years of experience for telling stories, I moaned about Ray's tone of voice when telling his stories.

I explained, 'Make your voice softer and quieter. Don't get too excited about the events. You are trying to put them to sleep, not to keep them up.' Ray couldn't help himself. He has a loud strong voice. He would sound as if he was shouting, even though we might be having a relaxed conversation. Rachel had her own taste of things. She loved anime, and she very rarely watched Disney movies, unlike Sarah, Rebecca and me. It was all Naruto and Japanese cartoon movies for Rachel. She even learnt some Japanese words and phrases from watching Naruto. Sarah and Rachel had this in common. I had lost count of how many times the two of them had watched the movie *Spirited Away*.

Having a second baby was a much easier journey. By then, I was a qualified mother. Having the third one, however, was a different story. Yes, I had the skills to love and care for a new baby, but I think I underestimated how stretched I was. At times I would've been talking to or answering all three of my girls, all at the same time. I had a big house to look after. I worked full time as a lecturer. Every year I would have new subjects to teach and new software to learn. Last year's lessons would need to be updated. I only took six months of maternity leave for each of my three babies. Each time I went back to work, I wished I didn't need to. However, my salary was needed, and I thought of my work as a gift. The only regret I had was denying my girls home lunch and missing on many school plays as occasionally it was not possible to take time off work.

I loved being a mother. I gave it my all. Since Sarah was born, I believe I departed from my world, or I became invisible. My girls became my world. Our home was theirs before it was mine and their dad's. Throughout the years, we had endless sleepovers at the weekends or during the holidays. I loved hearing my girls and their friends' noise from playing and having fun. In every house we lived in, I made sure there was a room for the girls and their toys. When their friends were around, Ray and I would keep out of their way and stay in our bedroom. I would only leave my room when needed. Building their den was their top request. So, the dining chairs would become the walls; all the bedsheets would come out of the drawers and be thrown over the chairs to make a nice and spacious dwelling place. Their fun would extend to the back garden during warmer weather. Since we didn't have a pool, we would get the sprinkler out. Instead of watering the grass, the sprinkler became the source of much fun and loud noises as if they could only communicate by shouting. I would be in the kitchen, wishing for an invite to join them. If I did get asked, it would be only for a while since soon; they would realise how high and embarrassing my screams were when splashed with water. I could tell when my time was up. Sometimes the weather determined how long I stayed outside. If the sun wasn't out then, I would get cold, and I would go inside even though I would hear them calling loudly, 'Please come back.' Otherwise, I would join in and be annoyingly competitive.

Throwing water balloons at each other when the weather was kind was hard work for me but a brief running around chasing each other kind of fun. They would come with me to the corner shop to buy the little balloons. They were cheap and cheerful as they cost 50 pence for a bag. The balloons were thin, small and assorted in colour. Filling them up with water was a pain in the neck. Having a wide water tap made it hard for me to fit in the mouth of the balloon around it. Stretching the balloons a bit more often caused them to burst in my hands. I would be soaking wet, and the game hadn't started yet. They would be waiting impatiently for all the balloons to be filled with water. We would divide the balloons equally, and the fun would begin. They would chase each other and hopefully get the balloon burst on the back of each other. The end of the game was after a few minutes.

As toddlers, at times, paper became the source of our entertainment. I would cut A4 sheet white or coloured paper into thin and long strips, and we each get a pile. We would sit on the carpet and use the strips of paper to build our two-dimensional farm with many rooms. We had to use our imagination to make the trees. We would crunch a bit of paper, which would be a cow, and a smaller crunched paper would be another animal. Of course, they knew which little piece of paper represented which animal. I, however, tried to avoid remembering all of this. We would check each other's work, and sometimes one of them would suggest there was no need for this particular one of mine, the one which was a better version of theirs. The little creature would end up in the bin or being borrowed by them.

My three girls, and their friends, of course, loved the game of islands and crocodiles. I would throw the cushions randomly on the carpet, pretending to be the islands, and the carpet was swamped with crocodiles waiting for any little foot that was not on the cushion to grab and eat. So, everybody had to be standing on any of the cushions. Gradually, I would remove one cushion at a time, so space which they could stand on got squeezed with every cushion removed. If their foot touched the carpet, they were out. As they got older, their dad tried to join in, but he wouldn't last long. At times he kind of spoiled the fun. His best entertaining act was when they would put the music on and ask him to dance. Actually, it was more like moving parts of his body randomly. It really was so funny, no coordination whatsoever. He would freeze his lower part and move his hands in certain way which was anything but a dance move. If he decided to move the lower part of his body, having enjoyed himself so far, he would flick his hip to one side and stop, as if he forgot how the move was achieved or what should come next. He would try to repeat the move with no luck. It was comedy at its best. We had all agreed Dad was allowed to show off his dancing moves in our dining room and never outside the house.

I wish my memories of those amazing times would still be fresh and still vivid during my last weeks on earth. They would be the best way to depart this life with the three of them on my mind. Memories of when Sarah would be crawling fast and racing to reach me, wearing her knitted white top and red trousers; and of Rebecca sitting in the kitchen sink, having fun, playing with water hitting it hard with her little hands not realising she would get herself wet, and of Rachel wearing my high heel shoes, with only a nappy on, walking around the house, having piled all the knickers she could find around her neck pretending to have a fancy necklace on.

While my girls were toddlers, I would never choose to put them on the floor or on a seat or a highchair during mealtimes. I had one arm for my child and the other arm for the rest of my duties. They loved it, and I loved it even more. My girls played together well, so although they are different and there is an age gap between the three of them, yet they entertained each other. I bet now they have their own stories to tell about their childhood.

I had my limitation, of course. My girls knew them, I knew them, and we didn't agree on this item of contention. I am an early bird, so I need to be in my bed before ten o'clock; otherwise, I don't function as a human. If they asked me to do anything after 10:00 pm, I would say, 'Sorry, I am switched off, gone to the land of nod.' I like my bath water very hot, so they soon gave up, jumping in my bath since they liked the water to be much cooler. I hate cleaning the mess after them being sick. I was very grateful to the three of them as even when they were little, they knew this weakness of mine, so every time they were sick, they would run to the toilet pan or to a bin in their room, which was much easier for me to clean. During a sleepover, one of Rachel's friends was sick in my bathroom, so every hand towel, bath towel and bathroom mats which were touched by it ended up in the bin. And once, when Rebecca was sick in the car when she was a toddler, we stopped the car, and everything was binned, even the child car seat. Unfortunately, I had to get rid of her favourite cream coloured little jacket, which made her look like a little lamb. Rebecca is twenty-two years old, and she is still annoyed at me for binning that jacket.

The one time that everybody was taken by surprise, and they still talk about it, involved baked beans. I was back from work, as usual, I had to pick Sarah and Rebecca up from after-school care, which was probably less than ten minutes' drive from home. Jenny, who was Rachel's childminder, would drop Rachel off at around 5:00 pm. It was one of those days that I knew I was so tense and tired. To my credit, I always enjoyed making good and healthy meals for my family, but this time, it was not one of those occasions. Having asked them what they want for dinner, I didn't have the ingredients to cook anything they suggested. I looked in the freezer, and there were only chicken dippers and chips. There were also green peas, which Rebecca liked, and a tin of baked beans, which Rachel liked. Sarah liked both; in fact, anything you put in front of Sarah, she would gladly take it. I could say for sure I had only served baked beans probably five times in my entire time as a mother. So, I said, 'How about chicken dippers with chips, peas, and baked beans?' None of them objected to my suggestion. I didn't have many other options, and dinner was sorted. I must've had a bad day at work, or some driver annoyed me during my twenty miles drive from work. Once dinner was ready, it was placed on the dining table, followed by 'Dinner is on the table.' I went to my room to get changed. I heard their footsteps going to the dining room. It is always a nice feeling when you are wearing comfy clothes, dinner on the table and the day's work is almost over. I went to the dining room to join my girls and have my dinner. I honestly couldn't recollect what happened, but all I could see was the flaming baked beans everywhere, on the carpet, on the side of the table, on their clothes and on the radiator. I am ashamed of myself as the scene had left a big impression on all of us. It gets mentioned every time we have a visitor. I hate cleaning, and especially when baked beans and their red sauce were all over the place, so I said to my girls, 'I can't deal with this.' And left the dining room and went to my room. No shouting, no arguing, no questioning who did what, just a simple retreat.

Much later that evening, when their dad came home, he was told what had happened. Knowing how fussy he was about his carpet, he switched into a cleaning mode straight away, although the girls had cleared most of the mess. Even today, we agreed to disagree on who did worse. I was defeated, admitting the lack of my skills for clearing the mess, and they were shocked for being abandoned by me.

God has always been good to us, and I know that He has an angel assigned to each of my girls as I don't think I could've looked after them on my own without His help. Prayer was almost always on my lips. At times it would've been the phrase "please Lord", repeated so many times, knowing that my Father knew what I was asking for. I always felt and said to those around me that when it comes to my relationship with my God, I would always say, pointing up with my index finger, 'Me and Him are okay, no matter what.' I never ever doubted His continuous provision to me and mine, always in time and always sufficient.

Life was much easier for me when the girls were young. Decisions were made without being discussed. They were carried out and completed, and then I would move on to the next thing without any questioning or arguing. When the girls got older, everybody had an opinion and fought for it, and each one of them would want to win any argument we had. I always lost whether we end up doing what I suggested or not, as it would always break my heart when I witness the bickering and the arguing, seeing them getting upset and losing my importance to them. I would complain to myself, 'Why can't they do as I tell them like it used to be when they were younger?' At times I started doubting myself and my opinions. On various occasions, it was embarrassing for me to admit when they were a bit older, their opinions were more plausible than mine.

Their taste in food used to drive me nuts. One of them liked mushrooms the other one hated it; one liked cooked tomato but not raw, the other one didn't like tomatoes at all; one liked her food mushed together, the other one didn't like the different items on her plate touching; salad had to go on a separate bowl for one of them while the other two would have the salad with the rest of the food; one of them liked to have tomato sauce with her chips the other two couldn't stand the smell of it. Each of them had favourite cutlery; I had to remember who liked which cutlery and not offer the specific cutlery to the other ones; one of them liked pizza, not any pizza, of course, the other one didn't; one of them liked all types of fish, the other one would only eat Salmon, while the third one would only eat Seabass; one of them liked Dolma, our traditional stuffed vine leaves meal, to be cooked very dry, the other two liked it wet and moist with lots of thick sauce at the bottom of the pot; one of them liked my version of pancakes the other one preferred having them made with Bananas. I am leaving out their varied taste in fruits, nuts, sausages, bacon, fried eggs or boiled eggs, etc., etc.

One of them liked food and lots of it, the other one didn't, and even after many reminders, she would still leave half of her food on the plate. What made it worse for me is when I got fed up asking the one who didn't eat to finish her food, the other one, having already cleared her plate, would say, 'Could I have it?' So when I don't remember who liked what, they appeared to be surprised and annoyed at me for not remembering all the above details and much more.

They would start, 'How many times I have told you I don't like whatever.' What happened to those days when I cooked one meal with the ingredients I chose, and all the three of them ate it with no fuss?

The same applies, of course, to gifts, so nowadays when buying Christmas presents, birthday presents or any other presents, nobody likes my presents. The three of them had decided I am not included anymore. They would choose the gifts for all the five of us from all the five of us. This arrangement, of course, I accepted, less hassle for me.

Rebecca's dream was always to visit New York. Her desire for visiting New York was made even greater when she started watching a crime drama television series called The Sopranos. It was one of her top five favourite's series, and the main character, the father, was her favourite character. Many times, we would be in the dining room, and Rebecca would start telling me about different scenes of the show. She still had the poster of the Soprano father on her bedroom wall. She also has a second poster of him for the last movie he did, 'Enough said.' When Sarah graduated, she started saving money and so the first thing she spent her money on was to take Rebecca for a holiday to New York. Being as organised as she always had been, Rebecca had the trip under control. She, of course, made sure one of the items on their itinerary was a guided tour that took them through New York City and Soprano land in New Jersey. When she came back, she was telling me about the places she saw where various scenes from the show were shot, including the famous diner and much more. Rachel was under 16, and that was the excuse I said to her for not accompanying her big sisters. I don't think either of the older sisters wanted to take the responsibility of looking after Rachel, and since the trip cost a lot of money, they wanted it to be hassle-free. So, Rachel didn't go to New York. Her dream city has always been Tokyo, and yes, a year later, once Sarah saved enough money to go abroad again, this time it was with Rachel, and Tokyo was their destination.

When Sarah and Rebecca were away to New York, I had the pleasure of Rachel's company, and so for the first time, it was only the two of us and abroad. We didn't, of course, go to New York, but we went to Grand Canarias. We left Ray home with his books, and in his opinion, he got the best deal.

Our apartment was in Puerto Rico. The journey on the coach from the airport to our apartment took forever. We literally were the last group to be dropped off. We arrived well after midnight. We were so tired. We had a quick shower and went to bed. The next morning, we explored our self-catering apartment, and we loved it. The flat had a beautiful sea view. The only issue we had was with the location of the complex where we stayed. It was up on a very high and steep hill, so high at times it felt we could touch the clouds. There was a winding path that took us all the way down to the beach. So, our first morning, we thought we would walk down, and since the fridge was empty, we could do some food shopping. I had brought with me tea bags and a few snack bars, which we ate for breakfast. After this holiday, I had decided never again I would agree to stay in a self-catering apartment. If you go for a holiday, you go to have a break from everything; especially, shopping, cooking and cleaning.

Walking down for food shopping was very exhausting. Rachel and I were physically near dead by the time we got back up to our apartment. As we started our walk down in that heat, I started worrying about the journey up. I kept this info to myself. I kept distracting Rachel by telling her to look at the amazing view, and it really was. The sun was blazing, and because we were so high up, the sea looked so much closer, simply magical views. Rachel took lots of photos with her mobile phone. We were told the journey from our apartment down to the small supermarket was a five-minute walk. It wasn't. There were some really steep sections, but for the most part, the path was okay and doable. There were many big trees along the way, which provided a nice cooling shade. All the trees were of the same type. They were covered with the most stunning orange blossom. So, I would look ahead of Rachel to judge how far away the next tree was, our next shelter from the heat.

We managed to get all the way down to the supermarket without stopping to catch our breath. The supermarket was much smaller than what we expected, and for each item we picked, we both were aware of the journey up. So, we discussed each item, definitely needed? Or not? As I was packing the shopping at the checkout, I arranged the items in four carrier bags, two bags each. It was time to head up to face what was the most heart pumping, sweat producing, feeling sorry for ourselves exercise. The journey up, to say the least, was very challenging. As we were staggering up, we had the chance to pay attention to the street. Taxis were going up and down the street, and yet we didn't have a clue totally immersed with the problem at hand. We continued the journey telling ourselves this was the last time we would climb up the road on foot. After a wee while, we arrived at a car park, so we dropped our shopping bags on the floor to have a rest. We chose the shortest path through the car park, as we continued our self-inflicting and self-roasting in the sun walk. As we kept going up, the frequency of our breaks increased. At some point, we couldn't count up to 50 steps before we stopped for our next breather. I said to Rachel, 'Darling, think of this walk as if we've been to a gym.' Not so smart thing to say; perhaps I had put her off the gym for good. The view was always amazing and kept us going. Rachel was so tired this time her mobile phone stayed in her pocket.

She would ask, 'Could we stop?'

And I would say, 'Just a few more steps.' A few minutes later, I started suggesting we stop for a break rather than waiting for her to ask for it. I took the two shopping bags off her, the light ones, as she was getting tired. She didn't object. We continued walking, this time without talking. Soon we were nearing the end, as we reached the corner where our apartment was. The minute we got inside, Rachel ran to the shower, and I did the same after her. We laid on the bed and enjoyed the well-deserved ice cream we bought. We each had two. It tasted the best ever. Since each time we walked down to the beach, we gladly paid the two euros for the taxi driver. The holiday was a great success in every way, but I still don't agree with myself for letting Rachel swim in the ocean. Even now, every time I visualise her in the dark deep navy-blue water with only her head sticking out, it terrifies me. What if she was stung by a jellyfish or another sea creature? What would I have done? I hated water, and I couldn't swim. Yet for Rachel, it was the highlight of her holiday.

I made an honest mistake by not checking whether our apartment had air-conditioning or not. So, although the apartment had a sea view, and we benefited from the sea breeze, inside the apartment was unbearably hot. The first night we arrived, we were so late, and we were so exhausted.

Rachel didn't fuss or question my decision to keep the veranda door open. I persuaded her by suggesting I would stay up all night to guard her in case there were any intruders!

During the second night, I said to Rachel, 'Darling, could we leave the veranda door open at night?'

Her reply was short and sweet. 'No way!' Rachel was terrified of intruders. She reminded me of when I was her age and the fear which crippled me when hearing dogs barking in the middle of the night.

So, I said, 'Why don't we create our own defence structure and place it right at the entrance of our apartment, where the veranda was. And if any stranger dared to come inside, he would be caught in our amazing trap?' She continued reading her book. I am not sure if she heard me or she just chose to ignore me. Thinking back about it now, who would climb eight floors to come inside our apartment? I wanted to have a good night's sleep, and so my creative mind got switched on. I looked around the living space to figure out what I could use. There was the coffee table, two living room chairs, four dining chairs, plus the plastic chairs on the veranda. I checked the rest of the flat and our suitcases for anything I could use as a rope to assemble the furniture together. I wanted to build a structure that would be too high and too wobbly to climb over it without tumbling down and crashing the furniture. What was I thinking of? I don't know. Although Rachel was totally immersed in her book, I got her attention eventually. She started suggesting we put this chair here, and tie this bit here, and bring the other chair on this side, and turn this one upside down. We were so creative we ended up with this hideous structure, which was so high and shapeless. We thought otherwise. We were impressed with our genius design. The veranda door was left open at night, and I had a great night's sleep. The next morning, it was a tedious undertaking to try and untangle the monster thing back to chairs to sit on.

When it was night-time, Rachel said, 'I don't think we need to do this again.' I agreed and changed the subject quickly in case she changed her mind. For the rest of our stay, the veranda door was kept open during the night.

I booked us into many day trips, and each one had its fun element. The best one was a guided tour. On the coach, which collected the fellow tourists from various hotels, was an old lady, chubby and short with a wobbly walk. She had her grandson with her, who had a similar age to Rachel. The old lady and her grandson were Spanish. The tour guide was a young man who knew his stuff. We learnt so much about the history of the various places we stopped at. The old lady added so much of her charm and wit, which made the trip far more memorable and enjoyable. She was such a character. She would interrupt the tour guide, so frequently, and start another version of whatever he was saying. She was louder and more confident than him. She kept talking over him. Her voice would get louder and faster when the topic at hand interested her. Nobody seemed to bother about her attitude. Rachel and I thought it was pure comedy. I noticed Rachel laughing even more when she and the grandson laughed at the grandmother's constant interruption simultaneously. At times, when the grandmother was being in her good behaviour and kept quiet for a bit, yet she would still attract attention by nodding her head continually and say, still loudly, 'si', which I believe is the word "yes" in Spanish. She repeated the word "si" with every node. This happened when she agreed with the information given by the tour guide. I really admired the man's patience and professionalism. He never lost his temper or said a word. Because the old lady couldn't walk as fast as the rest of us, this gave the guide a head start. He would say quickly what he wanted to say, with no interruptions for a while, until she arrived. She would sit at the most prime position and resume her version of the speech. At times she was talking to herself, as nobody was paying attention to her. I think she must've enjoyed herself. I am not sure about the rest of the tourists, but Rachel and I thought it was hilarious.

I lost touch with my friend Choona for decades. I always had hoped to see her again one day. I kind of guessed everybody had left home. I had asked my sisters about her, but nobody knew which country she had immigrated to. One day, I was over the moon when I had a phone call from her. We were both in our fifties. She said, 'I don't believe it is you.'

I replied, 'Same here.'

She said, 'I saw your cousin Rosa in the church last Sunday, and I asked her for your phone number.'

I said, 'I am so glad you did, as I always wondered what happened to you.' Then I said, 'You have no idea how many times I have seen you in my dreams.' One minute we were laughing, and the next minute we would start a sentence, and then we would pause for a while, as we would tear up, and then continue chatting. We went through so many stories of our shared lives. Our conversation had no structure, no order and no patience for each other. We would start talking about an incident so randomly and quickly, and while still talking, we would start another story that came to mind. I suppose being in our fifties, we were always fearful of forgetting what we were planning to say. To my disappointment, she did not remember the big white cockerel, double cake, imagine that, even Rachel knows double cake.

Today, Choona is living in Canada, married to an Italian man and with two teenage sons. Her fate and her siblings' fate mirror mine. Luckily, she had many of her siblings settled in Canada. A year after the amazing initial contact with Choona, she phoned me, but this time it was during a gathering you only could witness once in a lifetime. One of Choona's sisters, who has settled in Germany, had finally made the journey to Canada. She was meeting all her siblings and her mum, now in her eighties, for the first time in over twenty years. They all met in their mum's care home. They all took a turn to speak to me on the phone. So, although I wasn't present in the flesh, however, I did share the magical and momentous event as the phone was on speaker. We were on the phone for nearly an hour. I even heard their reactions when exchanging gifts. The noise, the child-like excitement, the pure joy, and for once, life was kind to Iraqi people.

Chapter 20
The Little Sparrow

As Ray and I have journeyed our lives together, I am always filled with gratitude for his companionship. I am convinced my God chose Ray, for the qualities he has, to become a great father for my girls. His input in their lives increased and deepened as they got older. Ray and I are very different in every way, but we complement each other beautifully. Sometimes, I wonder if we were living on the same planet and if we were listening to the same conversation. I would resign and accept his opinion, and at times, I would shake my head and smile. Ray is a very hardworking person, very smart and solid. He is my rock and my girls' idol. The three of them adore him. When I was younger, I was less mature in my attitude, and being so different from Ray, caused a lot of friction between us. I didn't get him, and he didn't get me.

I have to think really hard to come up with something that we both agree on. We are different in everything, our taste in people, movies, songs, objects and food. I like my breakfast cereal to be filled with nuts, seeds and fruits. Ray, on the other hand, like his plain. Preferably Kellogg's with nothing with it. I don't like meat; he loves his meat. When we all finish our meal, and as we are clearing the table, I might be tempted to pick any vegetables left on any plate; Ray, on the other hand, would be looking for any piece of bacon or other meat the girls didn't finish off. And if I cook a vegetarian meal, he would grumble quietly, asking for the real grub. I am so random and abstract in my way of thinking and behaviour, while Ray is so much a product and process person. He would not stop until he gets the job done and done properly. I, on the other hand, get impatient. I would try and get the job done as quickly as possible. When faced with a situation, I would say, 'Let us do it now.'

Ray would say, 'Let us think about it.' You would often hear him saying, 'Don't rush me.'

Ray worries too much about big things and little things while I would say, 'What is the big deal?'

I would like to go for day trips or short holidays, nothing extravagant, of course, while Ray would say, 'Let us just look at the pictures and pretend we are there.' I once made him come with me and the girls to the local swing park. After many arguments and discussions, he agreed to come. To my horror, on arriving, he opened the car boot and took his books out, thinking he was going to sit on a garden bench and get on with more reading. The girls and I won the argument, and so the books stayed in the car boot.

I am an early bird. I like doing the thinking, the planning, and any house chores first thing in the morning. He, however, was a night owl. This meant, of course, I was tired at night, and I would want to go to bed early while he went to sleep, probably after midnight. He would want to watch a movie or a repeat of a football match, while in my head, I would be saying, 'Why waste your time?' I am not allowed to sit near him when he is watching a football match. Once I gave him my interpretation of what happened during a football match, and since he said I spoiled it for him! He would be so focused on watching the ball like a hawk, and with every movement of the ball, he would move his body in the direction of the ball. There was no point talking to him because he won't hear anything. Throughout the match, he would be running his own commentating service for himself. He would critically comment on each player, each ball kick, any decision made by the referees, and even at times criticise or agree with what the professional commentators were saying. I worried about his wellbeing and his heart as he got so tense, his face and neck turn to a deep red colour. He needs to be reminded to breathe. He even forgets to enjoy the moment when a goal gets scored. He would rather wait till the end of the match as anything could happen at any moment. My interpretation of the magic of watching football is having twenty-four grown-up men running around like idiots chasing a ball, going from one side of the pitch to another. Then there were three referees, one of them was constantly trailing behind the idiots who were running after a ball. It is even funnier for the other two referees as they would be running along the side-line, up and down, up and down, pause for a bit, run again and guess what, following the ball as well and for nearly two hours. Imagine if you had a video clip showing only one of the side-line referees having removed the rest of the content engaged in a senseless movement for two whole hours. Now consider the thousands and thousands of the crowd standing way back, in freezing weather or in the rain still; maybe at times with their umbrellas up, from a distance watching a tiny ball going from one side to another chased by twenty-five grown-up men. To make the matter worse, they even get emotional about the ball; they clap hands, they jump up and down excited for a little ball that went a certain way. They even sing for the ball. All this waste of time, of course, is not for free; oh no, they pay well over 50 pounds probably for one ticket. And if it was four of them that was two hundred pounds just for the tickets. Then there was the travel cost. What about parking and the hassle of leaving the stadium after the match was over. And if this affair took place once a year, perhaps twice a year, they could be forgiven.

My main objection is how the human mind works to exploit any opportunity to make money. Why was it allowed for a footballer to earn millions? Why did we place such inflated value on football far more than any other decent worker does? Why didn't they get paid a salary just like the rest of us? Why not use the money generated to improve education, our hospitals, and our streets and inject money into hundreds of projects in need of funds? One of my colleagues at work has been to every home and away from his team's matches since 1970. He has even visited Eastern European countries in the seventies just for a football match, yet his wife does not have a dishwasher in her kitchen. How about if for one year only, every person involved in football get a similar salary to an average worker, still a decent salary and the money generated could be used to regenerate Africa! Imagine if aliens from the galaxies above were watching what goes on during a football match! What would they think of us and how we use our brains? Now you know why Ray didn't like me near him when football is on.

If I told you God made an animal speak, you would say 'no way.' But, of course, He did. There is a passage in the Bible from the book of Numbers where God made a donkey speak. I don't claim to have heard a donkey speak, but my God used another animal to speak to Ray and me. God used a little sparrow. Although many birds of different shapes and sizes visit my back garden, God chose one of the smallest birds to reach out to Ray and me. He chose a little sparrow.

One of Ray's known traits is he thinks too much and for too long, and therefore, he wastes his time worrying about things for too long. Even before he starts a job, he had decided in his mind this is going to be a mammoth job. Being a father of three girls, Ray ends up doing all the DIY jobs in the house. We are not sexist, or anything but truth has to be told, my three princesses and their queen mother would rather if these responsibilities were left to Ray. Unlike me, he would take his time, and what could've been completed in one hour with Ray, it would take at least four hours. He is a perfectionist. He would research each task for a long time, and he would get all the equipment he needs. In my opinion, Ray is Amazon's favourite customer. At times, we lose count of how many parcels he gets delivered on a weekly basis, mostly, of course, for his DIY work. Also, he is a regular customer of the local Screwfix shop. I know because I drive him there. When Ray is in his element, you might even hear his thoughts, totally immersed, almost cut off from the outside world. He always delivers, of course, always finishes every task so meticulously. Ray is so gracious and generous with his time, serving and completing every DIY job, even when he has never done it before.

My kitchen window is my doorway to heaven. It looks onto a hill, which is the ground of a golf course. The views from the kitchen window are simply beautiful, no matter what the weather is like. It is an amazing picture painted by my

God. It changes every second as the clouds move or as the weather changes in the four seasons. The most stunning views are when everything is covered with snow. In autumn time, however, the brown colour of tree branches and tree trunks get covered with little snow or frost. This gives the tree a beautiful shade of pink, so magical, nothing like it. You will be sure to see a few golfers, in all weathers, which gives the view a life of its own.

One Saturday morning, Ray and I were standing in our kitchen, shoulders touching, gazing at the beautiful view from our kitchen window and leaning on our kitchen worktop. He said with a deep and long sigh, with a tinge of desperation while looking at the gutter of the garage, 'Just look at the gutter; it is filled with moss. How am I going to clean it all?' The garage is situated on the right-hand side of the back garden. We got a good view of the top of the garage from where we were standing. The kitchen is a floor higher than the back garden. Ray doesn't like heights, but I make it even worse for him as I remind him of people we both knew who had either died or got seriously hurt from falling off a ladder. Cleaning the gutter was a job for him, and so he was feeling sorry for himself. I would usually insist on hiring a workman to do certain jobs. But somehow, this one wasn't too high. Besides, I would be around to help. The look on his face said it all, the familiar look which proceeded a big chore.

So, I said, 'Please don't worry, it will be okay. God will make a way. You worry too much.' This usually was my way of defusing situations when I couldn't think of an alternative. I continued, 'We could hire somebody to do it.' He disagreed. We went quiet for a minute or two, both looking at the gutter and wondering about the dreaded task ahead of Ray.

He continued, as if he had the weight of the whole world on his shoulder, 'I still have to correct the two chapters, one of my students had posted last week. The deadline for my paper is the end of the month. And I promised my parents I was going to visit them soon. I don't know when I will find time to clean the gutter.'

While we both were gripped in an apprehensive and overactive thinking zone, a little sparrow appeared. I have to say our back garden is too big for my liking. It is surrounded by huge old trees and bushes. So, it was a sparrow, not any other bird but a sparrow, which is probably one of the smallest birds to visit our back garden. The sparrow rested its little feet on the far end of the gutter. This was no ordinary sparrow. It was like a warrior with a great mission. I can't refer to it as an "it" because I know it was an angel sent from above in the body of a sparrow. I said to Ray, 'Look, Ray, look at the little sparrow.' The sparrow started from one end of the gutter, picking the moss with its little beak and dropping the moss in the garden, not on the roof of the garage but the other side, in the garden. The sparrow started from one end and never stopped till it reached the other end, clearing all the moss in its way with the precision of an unbelievable machine. I said to Ray, 'Look what God can do, and you were worried about clearing the moss.' We both were speechless and immensely humbled by God's provision. We stood there in wonder. I reflected on what we witnessed and asked so many questions 'Why wasn't it any other bird but a little one with a little beak and little feet?' Why did the sparrow appear in that moment and not later on when we had left the kitchen? Why didn't it stop till all the moss was all cleared, so methodically, as good as Ray would have done it, if not better? Why was it done after Ray's sighs and the way he showed his weakness? Why didn't the sparrow throw the moss on the roof of the garage but on the garden, so the job was completed perfectly? I believe God was in the kitchen that morning, listening to our chat. I believe He showed up in a sweet and instant kind of teasing way of communication. A kind of supernatural intervention that touched our hearts and solved Ray's problem. I said to Ray, 'Although you are a great DIY person, I think the little sparrow did an exemplary work.' He agreed.

So, it happened, a new and a bright chapter started as both our extended families had finally left Iraq and trod a new path in their later life as they found new lands across the continents to settle in. Life was fairer to some more than others. Each family had new struggles and challenges as they tried to fit in the neighbourhood; they ended up living in. Major changes in later life, imposed by circumstance, are not an everyday occurrence. You are never prepared for massive upheaval in life like this with all that it entails. It is a shock to the system with a new culture, different weather, a new language and a whole new community to get used to. Everything you have known and became accustomed to has now transfigured into a new existing. With each passing day, the thought of going back home became a distant wish, watching their children enjoying the many opportunities as they were granted a new lease of life. My youngest brother-in-law ended up in California and the middle one in Canada, not just any part of Canada but in the far north where the temperature plummets to sub-zero degrees. During the cold months, the temperature could reach minus $40C^{o,}$ and you could get frostbite in minutes, and if you forgot yourself outside, you would freeze to death. So much contrast to the weather that my youngest brother-in-law enjoyed in California as I have been told it is around 20C° for most parts of the year. The rest of my in-laws lived in Britain, so Miriam had finally retired and left the education system of Iraq after forty-six years with no pension or any appreciation for the length of her mammoth years of service.

We had one in a lifetime event during Christmas of 2008. Like birds flying back to their nest, I found myself welcoming all my in-laws in my house. It was such a joyous occasion. There were eighteen of us. The children had a sleepover every night. Every room in the house had an inflated bed on the floor at night-time, including the dining room. Mealtimes were all changed. We ate when whoever was hungry. Sometimes breakfast was served three times a day. Grocery Shopping was done every day. The dining table was the focal point, and it was well utilised. There was so much to catch up with. It was strange how the five brothers were coming from the same family, yet because of settling in new countries, they ended up experiencing a different way of living. Many stories were told and shared as to how the same thing was done differently. Our children's accents were different, but we were grateful that they all spoke English and so they could communicate with each other. Christmas had to be different a bit, a mixture of the tradition plus newly adopted practices. The weather during this time of the year was good, in my opinion. Winter in Scotland, yet it did not snow, and the temperature stayed above zero for the two weeks. However, this was not good enough for the Canadian of us, and it was definitely not good for the Californian residents. The Canadian brother-in-law kept saying, lifting his T-shirt up, 'It is too hot in here. I am boiling. Please open the windows.' He was wearing shorts and a T-shirt the entire time. He would go out to the back garden to escape the heat.

As for the Californian one, he would follow by saying, 'What are you doing? It is freezing in here.' He would shut any opened window. He was constantly occupied by going after his two little boys holding their thick winter jackets, urging them to put their jackets on, not forgetting to pull the hoods up. As for me, I just kept smiling, shaking my head and letting them sort the weather issue amongst themselves. The one person who enjoyed this gathering most was Miriam. She looked like a queen, and I am sure she felt like a queen. Before everybody left and returned to their new countries, my freezer was filled with traditional Iraqi food that only my Canadian brother-in-law has mastered the craft of making them.

Looking back at my life, and as my little girls are now three wonderful and beautiful young ladies. They are my crown with which I adorn my head with. I came to accept; however, I was only made to function as a mother of young little girls. Being a middle-aged lady, I can't escape the feeling of being made redundant. Since Sarah's birth, I was lost to myself. I lived for others. My little girls were at the centre of all my decision making. No matter where I was, hearing the word "mum" would instantly cause me to reply, 'Yes, my darling,' forgetting my girls weren't even with me.

Nowadays, when I hear little girls shout to their mums, 'Mum!' I would smile to myself with tight-lipped and a lump in my throat fighting the glassy watery eyes I end up with. Life has lost its taste and its lovely smells. Today, I have been converted into a huge old and flaky plant. Instead of getting the essential daily dosage of water and light, it is left in a dark corner seizing the sporadic little drops which come its way now and then. Little drops of water end up evaporating straightaway on its dry surface.

The back garden is deserted, and it appears even bigger without its occupants running around, at times with their idiot mother joining in. Except, presently, for a family of foxes, the new residents. They would sunbathe early morning on sunny days, confident of no children around to disturb their lazy and leisure time. I would watch them, a bundle of red, lush and shiny fur, head almost hidden, tucked in the soft and warm wrap. I have marked the holes in the back garden, which led to their underground burrows. Early mornings, I would be standing in my kitchen, in the same spot I used to stand watching my little girls chasing each other. Instead, I might catch the playful little cubs chasing each other, darting in circles, tumbling down while baring their teeth at each other rowdily. These naughty little creatures have even stolen dirty little balls from other houses and carried them to my back garden. I am left with a new kind of decision to make, should I bin the dirty stolen items or should I leave their toys alone? Life is dull without my little girls, day follows another day, and word follows another word, probably the same words too. Nothing changes here. In fact, it shrinks rather than it increases, and the mind closes on itself again. No sleepovers, no birthday parties, and no parents' night visits to the school. Same seasons, same leaves, same changes of colours, same little meals to cook, and same little mess to clear. My earlier life has disappeared. I am chasing after the world it has been created for me, and with every backward step I am taking to go back to it and relive it, I feel it has developed wings to speed away from me. Every day passes, I am dropping off a few treasures from my memory store. Time is pulling me out of that magical zone, but I am forcing myself back into their childhood years. I am chasing the wind, dust and dry leaves around me, passing by me, lifting my memories and leaving me empty.

Gazing at old photos, little faces at various ages. Every corner in the house is filled with them, every cell in my brain, photos of cheeky smiles and cuddles, wrapped myself around my little girls as if someone is going to snatch them away from me. I go from one room to another, living and then reliving those moments captured in these images. I yearn for a cuddle, but I get none. I hear faint chats in my head, but I don't recognise any voices, the start of an incomplete sentence muddled with the end of another sentence. Nowadays, only my ears hear my words, and only my lips taste my food in an empty world of deafening silence. One day, I thought I was the tree of my family; today, I am a broken and dry autumn leaf gasping for air and aching for a kind touch from the young and the living. I am one of the many millions of parents who survive the empty nest syndrome.

Chapter 21

My Mum

My life taught me most mothers are precious, but my mother was extra precious. Being the sixth of her seven children, I know I didn't have all her love solely for me, but she gave me my share of her love, and it was sufficient. I take comfort in knowing no matter what I did or said, her unconditional love covered all my failings, and her purity and goodness cancelled all my faults. Her physical presence in my life stopped on my wedding day, but her spirit never left me.

Everybody has a story to tell. And here is my story. I was young and naïve, then I got married, and that was the end for my mum and me. My mother and I never saw each other since. Twenty-three years later, her body had enough of this world. During these years, I was alive yet absent. My mum and I got older to the people around us, yet to each other, we stayed looking the same. Time and space didn't matter. Mum and I lived thousands of miles away. Life cheated us. Throughout my life, I knew my mum was pleased with me. She masked my weaknesses with her love and understanding – simple words, deep meaning and pure love, nothing more and nothing less.

Every time I thought of Mum, my eyes started a continuous loop of scanning images from the past, some silent ones and some with words and conversations which I could vaguely remember. At times, I wished I could disappear to a place where no one had ever been before. Only then could I open my eyes so widely, getting rid of the fluff blocking my ears; the black and white which had forever engulfed me, like a shell, it would evaporate, and out I would come. No borders, no barriers, no fog and no grey colours, just purity. I would run forever. I would fly forever; I would dance forever to sounds nobody could hear. Freely and aimlessly, I would glide like a tiny dot in space. Are you listening, Mum?

My mum's face was like another layer added to my eyes. I saw it no matter where I was – the words of Psalm 23 ring in my ears to accompany the presence of my mum's face. Every word of the Psalm was written for my mum. My mum and I were like two pieces of one page, torn and blown away by the wind to the opposite corners of the earth. We never had the chance to reunite again. But we were together, always. Although our paths had parted, we were linked forever as if the cord at birth was never cut.

I am so sorry, Mum, for the pain, the discomfort and the extra workload my arrival to this world caused you. Were you pleased to hold me for the first time in your arms? I could picture your beautiful eyes looking down at me. I hope I never caused you any pain during the following years. I wish I had never asked you for things both you and I knew you couldn't afford to buy. I wish I had appreciated your presence when you were around. I wish I helped with house chores. I wish I had the opportunity to have you with me as you got older rather than picturing it all.

Questions

I was left wondering about your last day on earth, wishing you could hear me. Where do I start?

How was the night before you fell asleep for the last time?

Were you aware of it happening?

Were you aware of near of the end kind of being?

Did you wish someone was holding your hand or holding your body?

Was your body aching, or was it totally numb?

How did it feel to finally let go?

What were the last thoughts which came to your mind?

Did you think of me?

Did you say my name? And if so, were you happy or sad?

I hope you didn't cry. I hope only happy memories filled your mind. I hope you were warm enough.

Were you hungry, Mum?

What was the last thing you tasted or ate?

Which part of the chicken was your share?

When was it the last time you tasted the breast of a chicken?

Was your plate always the last one to be served?

Was your bed comfortable?

Did you want your body turned, but you didn't have the energy to do it on your own?

What was the last thing you touched or held in your hand?

What were your last words?

How did you feel, Mum? Scared, alone, disappointed, rejected, or just blank?

Did you wish you had your sight back, only for a wee while to see your children had returned and gathered around you?

Did I come to your near-final thoughts? I think you would've given up on waiting on me by then, still hoping but knowing both you and I could only dream about.

Is that why you left while you were asleep? I am so glad you did; at least, you didn't feel so alone and forgotten about. Was it time to go, Mum?

But I know you said your prayers, and perhaps you fell asleep while still praying.

I know you were filled with peace, which can only come from the Lord God almighty. And I know no matter what, you felt content because of Him, who was on your side. I know it was Him who was with you, His hand held your hand, His name you called last, His strength kept your body comfortable, His presence let you see your children, all of them flew back home to see you, His love filled your senses and His power let your spirit soar to your home in heaven. You would've said these scriptures, 'Naked I came from my mother's womb, and naked I shall depart. The Lord gave, and the Lord has taken away; may the name of the Lord be praised.'

On my way to work, I pass by beautiful hills. I used to picture myself sitting on these hills next to you, picking wildflowers together, and minding our own business, like two little fairies not disturbed by the outside world. When you passed away, I was left alone on these hills: puzzled, looking around, searching for you, Mum, and knowing I will never find you.

When my Sarah was about to come to this world, and when the labour pain started, I called for you. How I wished you were with me. It was the same with Rebecca's and Rachel's, still wishing! I cried for you whether I was happy or sad, wishing I could share what I was going through with you. My wish never came true, so I started whispering it instead. I was growing up without you, Mum. Today, the little girl of yours had turned into an old lady, who never stopped missing you.

I bet you never wished for me to be with you. You wanted me to stay far and away. And whenever I came to your thoughts, you were glad that I was not sharing your wretched life with you. You were comforted knowing I was happy and well-fed. But every time you came to my thoughts, it was like opening the cut again, the wound which never healed. My mum was living in agony, and I couldn't change a thing. I wonder if you did not wish to have been deaf as well as blind. Somewhere, so far away, lay your beautiful bones, so alone and so unnoticed. Did anyone bring flowers to your resting place? Do you get any visitors? Of course not. You who raised up seven children and had eighteen grandchildren, yet you have no one to visit your beautiful bones. Life is so unfair, Mum; life is so unfair.

Since I left home and was away from you, I found it hard to enjoy food, knowing you were missing out. I would tell myself I wish this plate would fly away, and somehow it got placed in front of you. And would somebody, very kindly, bring your hand and guide it near the food and let you enjoy it. Every time I had a nice warm shower, I would think of you and wish your body was the one getting washed. Every time I would look at the beautiful trees and the amazing nature through my car window, as I drive to work, I would remember you and whisper to you, 'Mum, I am looking at these beautiful scenes for you and me.'

Nothing changes, Mum; you were always the last on everybody's list, including yours. We weren't neighbours or anything, you never visited me, or entered my house, or had seen my girls, no, none of that. I was denied all of it. I never had the chance to cook a nice meal for you and find out whether you liked my cooking or not, take you to the shops maybe, cut your toenails, do the shopping for you, walk you to the park, drive you to the seaside, moan to you about anything and everything, watch a TV program together why not, no, none of that. You and I, Mum, never had the chance to be together, not since I got married. It is not a long time; it is a lifetime. I am well, and all is well with me. That is all I ever heard you say on the phone. Was it though, Mum? No, it wasn't, not really, it never was, but what could you have done? What could I have done? It was never well with you, Mum, and now it will never be well with me.

You are gone, robbed of your dignity and pride, and I am here, still living, robbed of my dignity and pride for the way my mum lived her life. I am so ashamed of myself and so utterly heartbroken for not having the chance to serve you, for not making it better for you, for my absence when you needed me most. What do I say when asked: how was it with you and your mother? How? All you ever heard my mum say about me was 'She is very kind.'

All you will ever hear me say about my mother is that 'There is no one like her.'

More questions

How did you plan your funeral, Mum?

How did you want your final journey to be?

Did you picture me amongst the crowd?

Did you hear my voice calling for you?

Did you hear my voice saying the prayers during your last mass?

Which dress did you want to be wearing?

Did you even have a dress good enough to be chosen for your funeral?

Did you smell nice?

Was your tummy empty?

Were you clean?

Was your skin nice to touch?

Were your perfect bones gently seen to?

How was it for you, Mum?

How was your last send-off?

Was it similar to the many funerals you had attended, with or without an invite?

Did you think there would be hundreds of people attending yours?

If you had a plan for your funeral, Mum, and whatever your plan was, none of it happened. You, Mum, had one of your seven children present, not even the rest of his family. Your other six children, each one of them was thousands of miles away, busy living their lives. As for me, three words reached over the phone the following morning to announce your departure. That is how I knew my beautiful mum had left this world, so alone, so weak, so cheap and so neglected but I bet so relieved.

Even though I silently cried for you, but my heart screamed so loudly, I am sure you heard it. And if you were to see who was laying your beautiful body in its final bed, because I wished so much to be there, you would've seen my face instead of the faces of the strangers who were present. My heart is aching, and my mind is so gone. Never again will I feel the same; never again will I be able to say I have a mum, and I am taking her out for dinner for Mother's Day. Not that I ever did. Still, I always dreamt about it every year, and now even dreams are too much to ask.

My beautiful and gracious mum, my kind and gentle mum, my poor yet worth the riches of the earth, my blind mum, blind to every badness but could only see goodness and beauty in everything and in everyone. Your beautiful bones must've got used to the harsh weather, the dampness, the loneliness, the darkness, and the ultimate silence. I love you, Mum; I love how this world doesn't have words fit to describe you but only things from the heavens above. You never belonged to this world, Mum. You came, and you left, and in between, you fulfilled every duty given to you with the ultimate sacrifice. You left, Mum, unnoticed, oh, but I bet the heavens was bursting with joyful cheering to welcome you back, His precious daughter and my loss.

Please forgive my failings.

Please forgive me for not being around when your weak body needed me most.

Please forgive me for not giving you your rightful place in my life.

Please forgive me for being the daughter who I will never be proud of.

Please forgive me for being wrapped up in my own life and forgetting about you as if you never existed. I am left with regrets, regrets which lay so heavy on my heart. I am bruised with terminal soreness, which is consuming me and will never leave me. I failed you, Mum, and I failed myself.

Chapter 22

Facts

In an ideal world, one in which war was not the ultimate decider and game-changer, I wonder what my life would have been like. War destroyed so much, tainted my life with sadness. During especially dark times, war depleted my desire to exist. War is a losing game. There are no winners. There are no war heroes. War took so much away. Before mobile phones became an everyday necessity, and before you could face message your friends and family across the world for free, phone bills were extortionate. During these times, life at home was desperate. British Telecom (BT) landlines or the phone boxes were the only means of contacting home. The cost per minute from a landline was £1.39, and from a phone box, it was £1.59. I dreaded getting the phone bill. Over £400 bill for three months would make my heart sink every time it arrived. For us, the £400 phone bill was a small fortune in those days. Phoning home was a bittersweet experience, hearing their voices to soothe the pain of missing them versus the hopelessness of their pitiful existence. I would argue with myself as to what was the point of phoning home. What were they going to tell me? Life was unbearable; there was a shortage of everything; power cuts and no running water were a daily occurrence, long queues for the little food, holding rations close to the chest. What would I say in return? Life was great; everything was available; the supermarkets were filled with food, and I was spoiled for choices; transport was great; people went on holidays; hospitals were open, staffed, and well equipped. How could I? There was nothing I could've talked about which they were not lacking. Nothing I could've shared, knowing in advance their experience was the opposite of mine.

Ordinary people would give up on the basics and sell whatever they could do in order to generate cash to buy food. Selling their homes' internal doors was one person's clever idea, which was copied by the rest. Many families gave up furniture, jewellery, even cutlery. Unfortunately, the hardship saw many siblings fall out over money; relationships broke up as everybody desperately wanted to grab the next penny available. The pitiful existence destroyed families and communities, and it caused the destitution of hundreds of thousands of innocent citizens. Every time I had the chance to speak to my mother, she would assure me with white lies. 'We are good, everything is fine, don't worry about us.' I knew it was not the case, but I would cowardly and hopelessly go quiet and awkwardly mumble, not knowing what subject to change our conversation. Once, and out of despair, my index finger pressed a button, and the phone call ended. I went to my room and cried bitterly.

The imposed miserable way of life got worse with each day passing. People would flee the cursed land as life became impossible. Uprooting and facing the unknown became the one wish on the mind of millions. Despite being heartbroken for the forced exodus, yet for security reasons, the multitude was denied saying their final goodbyes to those left behind. Out of fear, they would quietly and secretly leave. So was the case with my siblings, Ray's siblings, and their families. Gradually, one after another ended up leaving everything behind to grasp to life elsewhere. My sister, by now, a hospital consultant, had so much wealth, she employed a gardener, a nanny and a guard at the entrance of her mansion. No one could comprehend how much my sister struggled to build her life again, starting from the bottom. The bottom she did not even experience in Iraq. Of course, these facts are not considered in the world's accounts and records when calculating the cost of wars.

The imposed poverty troubled my father as he saw himself as a burden. By now, only Magdalene and my older brother were left in Iraq. During his last two weeks alive, my dad was asking for his children, yearning to see them. Magdalene kept coming up with one lie after another. 'They were here earlier. They came to see you, but you were asleep. They did not want to wake you up.' Or she would say, 'They cannot get leave.' My niece was at my father's side constantly. She embodied the love and the care of all his children in the presence of one little grandchild. During the last three days, my dad went into a coma. His weak body finally had enough as his organs gave up, one by one. He was done with this life. He was done with what his eyes saw.

The sad news of my dad's passing reached me through the phone. I was consoled by my mother; her loving words calmed my sore heart. I was living in Moulin Terrace at the time. I put the phone down and kept walking aimlessly from one room to another, my heart aching, and my tears flowing effortlessly. Death was final, and no matter what, I was never going to see my father again. I never doubted God's plan for my life, but the price I had to pay was too high. I never had the chance to see my dad throughout my adulthood life. To be on my own, thousands of miles away, meant I had nobody to share my grief with, and I could not attend my dad's funeral service. I could not take all the pain in. Why life had to be this hard?

Years after the invasion, the country went through even drearier years. Life became cheap. Neighbours turned against their neighbours for being from a different sect or faction. And everybody turned against Christians. Christians were considered allies of the West. Countless incidents happened on a daily basis as crime became the new norm. My mother, now in her late seventies, was left alone in our family home. My oldest brother, the last one left in Iraq, lived nearby. My mother could not and would not want to leave the country. She insisted on staying and dying in her house. She was hopeful, more like wishful dreaming, that life would go back to normal, and her deserted children would return back home. When queuing for food, made available through rations, my mum would get shouted at: 'This queue is not for the likes of you. Go and ask President Bush for your food.' The mood changed and what was morally unacceptable soon became acceptable. Life was a battle for survival. Theft, crime, and even killing for food was now ethically justified. You would not sell anything expensive as whoever you sold it to would soon pay you a threatening visit. The money would end up back with the buyer. My sister-in-law's brother made the mistake of selling his house as he was planning to leave the county, unlike the rest of my siblings who fled the country, leaving their properties and their furniture behind. Sadly, my sister-in-law's brother paid the ultimate price, his life and his wife's life at the hand of the buyers. The money from the sale of the house was gone during the night. The couple was found dead the following morning.

In 2007, my mum received a threatening letter asking her to leave her house, or she would be killed. She ignored it. A few days later, she received a second one – this time with obscene words as to what they would do to her if she did not comply. By now, my mother was almost blind. She could barely recognise her surroundings. Leave your house or else; this would have never happened in the past. Iraqi people, who I knew, were good, decent, and generous. They respected their elders. Where did this new breed sprout form? How could they stoop so low?

When faced with such depravity, what options did Mum have? My brother and his family took my mother and left the capital and headed up north. They were not allowed to take any of their belongings with them. No one should ever be treated this way. I was spared the details of their journey. Where was love? What more crimes was a man capable of committing when God was not present? My mother ended up living in a two-bedroom flat, sharing it with my brother and his family. How would you feel, my reader, if you were my mum or if she was your mum or your granny? How would anybody feel if this was happening on their doorstep? Yes, the invasion was over, the war was over, but at what human cost? What a mess was created and covered up with statements like 'Oh, but democracy was introduced.' What democracy? What outcome? Any evidence of democracy? What was achieved? Would those who made the decision for invading Iraq care to answer?

My mother started her life loving and giving. Like a mother hen, she was busy serving and providing. Yet the power of darkness did not miss her out. This was the beginning of the end of her time on earth. They were the darkest times of her life. The only comforting thought Mum had was her oldest son was still with her. My brother was a biology teacher, and it was not long before he found a job in a secondary school in one of the villages not far from where they ended up living. If you had asked Mum, 'Who of your seven children would you want to be with in your last year? she would have picked my big brother. My brother was a deacon in the church. Since Mum could not go to church anymore, my brother would conduct a church service just for her. I was not present, of course, but I know this would have been like a soothing balm for her soul.

My brother became my mother's carer in the last few months of her life. I was eternally grateful to him. I did my bit financially, and he did his best to keep her clean and comfortable. My brother's family did not stay up north long as they immigrated to Canada. My brother was left with my mum until she was gone. Although it was an unbearable ending to one remarkable lady, yet my mum never complained, always full of hope. During the last phone call I made to speak to her, she sang a few lines of a song for me, one which we used to sing during weddings and happy occasions. I tearfully joined in, whispering as I fought my trembling lips. She told me about the prayers which my brother would say or sing to her. By now, she started forgetting the words, even the words for the Lord's Prayer, the one which she must have prayed a million times during her life. Just before we finished the last call, she said to me,

'Will you come and see me?' In Aramaic, her exact words were, 'Petyat khaz yatty?' These words are tattooed in my heart, pierced like a dagger. Throughout the twenty-three years in which we were apart, she never ever asked this question or hinted at anything with similar meaning. These words sting me every day since. What was I meant to say?

I replied with the words 'bkhelad alaha', which translates to 'by the power of God'. We would use this phrase when, humanely, situations were impossible, but if God was willing, it could happen. Although we both knew it was never going to happen. And it did not. Two days after the phone call, my mum was gone, left this earth forever. My brother gave my mum a Catholic funeral service and buried her with the help of his students and fellow teachers. Soon after, my brother too left the county, the last one of my family to leave. He was reunited with his own family in Canada.

God works in mysterious ways, as after my mother had gone for her last sleep, much darker times descended upon the land. God's timing caused me to be speechless. Throughout history, many villages in the north of Iraq had been occupied by Christian families since they were visited by the Apostles in the first century, including the one my mum was buried in. In 2014, these villages were swept by ISIS (Islamic State of Iraq and Syria), the evil powers which demonstrated to the world new waves of depravity and practiced obscene new ways of torturing and killing people. I shudder to think: *what if my mum was still alive*? Isn't it madness to think I am uttering these words: 'I was at peace knowing my mother was gone? She was spared to die or live at the hands of ISIS. I am not sure which was going to be worse.' Yet again, the Christian families, many of whom had already fled to other parts of the country, had to find new places to escape to. So, they headed further up north. For many families, their new homes became the traffic islands, the pedestrian refuge space, which is a raised section of pavement between two lanes of traffic. How about this existence, my reader? Any justice here? Any words? You are excused to go numb, mind going blank and eyes staring in the distance. Was the outside world bothered?

Many Christian people around the world went out in the streets to show their solidarity and to bring to the attention of the world the plight of those whose life was destroyed and afflicted with never-ending torture. Many people wore T-shirts with the letter n in Arabic ن which symbolises being Christian. Nassara in Arabic means Christian. And in order to identify which houses belonged to Christians, ISIS fighters had painted the letter ن on the front wall of these homes. The families living in these homes were given three options, renounce your Christian faith, flee for your life, or your head will be chopped off. I had decided I was not calling Iraq "home" anymore. My heart turned into a stone. I blocked the news from that land totally out of my mind. Nothing more to say. All hope is gone for peace to return to that land in my lifetime. Probably in the far future, perhaps in fifty years' time. Who knows when life will go back to normal? I will not have the chance of a return visit to Iraq, but perhaps one day, my girls might visit my parents' bones for me if they could find them.

It seems to me the outside world does not understand any of these facts, or even worse it chooses to ignore them. What happened to my family's three generations is just a mist in the air. Their suffering does not matter. It does not matter if any

238

trace of Christian existence was wiped out tomorrow from Iraq, its Christian heritage was lost forever, and its people turned into ghosts. The world's leaders think the job is done and democracy was introduced. The suffering of millions of Christians of the Middle East does not matter. They are displaced yet again only God knows where to, forever strangers in whatever land they live in today. If you want to know, my reader, what this means then think about the phrase Post-Traumatic Stress Disorder (PTSD), which the world understands very well and is defined as a condition, an anxiety disorder caused by very stressful, frightening or distressing events. Multiply this by how many times you fancy, and then you will get what the world has inflicted on us. They say time is a healer, but time cannot wipe anything away. Time cannot bring anything back. Time cannot let you start again. Time keeps running, not caring about who and how people were left behind and wiped out.

I do not claim to be anything but a plain girl from a poor family whose life was influenced by circumstance, way beyond my abilities. My path was made for me as I was snatched away from my surroundings and dropped into a world that only higher powers would have designed for me. I believe despite all the badness I saw exhibited so undoubtedly on a daily basis, I believe my God rules over every situation. My life taught me to put my trust in God alone. I made Him my guide, and by doing so, many beautiful surprises awaited me – surprises and gifts which amazed me with their intensity and simplicity. I pray for you, my reader, for much power and strength from above to touch your life and put your mind at peace and carry you through your darkest hours. My life at times was so overwhelmingly difficult that I could have

239

choked with its pain and died. The one certain thing I have concluded is without my faith in my God, I can truly say my life would have been dark, empty, joyless, and short. I know my choices in life would have been influenced by a corrupt and destructive mind. The little things in my life, which gave me great joy, would have been missed out and ignored or even worse explained as coincidences.

I do not claim to know the word of God like the scholars who are privileged enough to study it on a daily basis. I know my vocabulary and my comprehension is limited, but I know without a shadow of a doubt that my God knows me inside out. He knows every breath and every sigh I take, every grieve I endured, every tear I shed, every bad thing and ill-thought I suffered. He knows my limitations, yet He thinks of me, the little me, as His inheritance. What a privilege and what an immeasurable joy to know I have had my little steps guided by my Father above.

I have learnt to claim my life through prayer, so in every moment of my life, I spoke to Him, He who made me, He made the universe, the great I AM, the one who no one can fathom, yet He is interested in every detail of my days. I do not know why He loves me, but one thing I know: without His love, I am the tiny dot of dust that does not belong anywhere or at any place, yet with His love, I am a conqueror. The little insignificant ant gets transformed into a unique superhero, all the DC and Marvel characters with their powers put together and turn into a real person inside me. With God beside me, I fear nothing, and I lack nothing.

Chapter 23

Land of Wars

Man's Way

I was made an emigrant twice in my lifetime, not by choice but by desperation, Turkey, Iraq, and then lost everywhere. When you watch a movie about the First and the Second World Wars; when you read a history book about wars; when you attend the yearly memorial services for the lives lost in the two wars; when the duly care, help and empathy are offered to war veterans; you will never hear any mention of what my grandparents, parents and my siblings had to endure. Our suffering is nowhere to be found. The price my grandparents, my parents, my siblings, and I had to pay is not grasped by many. We are still paying the price today and every day. Living strangers forever in the countries we ended up in, scattered in every continent in the world. Our children cannot communicate with each other as their grandparent's language is lost. Their first language is the language of the country where their parents have ended up living. I have nephews and nieces in their twenties who I have yet to meet. I never saw my parents since I left Iraq. I could never visit my parents' graves. No matter where I go or where I live, I will always be the lady with a different accent.

My parents had seven children. History repeated itself, and so for the reasons my parents were made immigrants, in their old age, they watched their seven children fleeing their place of birth for similar reasons. I lost home, my place of birth. How can I call it home when my mum was forced to give up what she considered her eighth child? In fear, an old, blind, and valueless widow, dragging her feet to the unknown, is a sight held against everybody who had anything to do with war – shame on this wretched world when man's way is pursued.

I am not alone, of course. We are the forgotten millions of Christian families from the Middle East. We don't interest the media. The politicians turn a blind eye to our plight. Even the church leaders don't see us as headlines' grabbing issue. In this twisted world, it seems some people matter, and others do not.

There is a land, for real, the Holy Bible refers to it as the garden of Eden, Genesis chapter 2:9 'The LORD God made all kinds of trees grow out of the ground – trees that were pleasing to the eye and good for food. There is more, Genesis chapter 2:12 'The gold of that land is good; aromatic resin and onyx are also there.' This land was good enough for the Lord God to place Adam and Eve to live in it. His first creation. What did Adam do? Well, you know the story. If not, then please read the rest of the book of Genesis to find out. It had plenty of water, a steady climate, and fertile soil. I have tasted the produce of the land. The quality of its crops, fruits and vegetables, there is nothing like it. They taste and smell good. I bet there are plenty of natural resources and minerals yet to be discovered. Mesopotamia, the cradle of civilisation, where the first cities in history were established, is the land of the first writing (Cuneiform), Astronomy and Law. The Code of Hammurabi is a well-preserved Babylonian code of law. The first poem written in history is to be found in the Epic of Gilgamesh, as a series of Sumerian poems dating back to 2100 B.C. The base 60 system for time and three hundred and sixty circular angles are a few of their advanced discoveries in Maths. Their innovation to study the sky, which the Greeks later adopted to create the Zodiac, started by dividing the year into twelve periods. They discovered the first wheel amongst endless other innovations in all areas, including healthcare, science, buildings and irrigation systems. The world authorities have not been kind to that land as not enough resources, and attention was given to discover its rich history.

Yet, a country which has been battered in the past forty years, destroyed by wars, sanctions imposed for many long years, cursed by sectarian fights, and ruled by corrupt officials. The land is poisoned, the course of the big rivers has been changed, natural resources destroyed, and their daily bread stolen. At times, we were made to feel ashamed to awkwardly utter where we are from; wrong guesses from the enquirer would have been a relief. For the ordinary people in the street, Iraq was to encapsulate everything which nobody wanted to associate with. A word not to be mentioned, a topic you do not want to be seen discussing. Even today, we would get irritated when asked, 'Where are you from?' Man's way turned the Garden of Eden into a land of wars.

Man's Doing

We were made to experience hell on earth. Mourners, while gathered for the funeral of their loved ones, killed by suicide bombers, found themselves attacked by yet another suicide bomber. The evil minds would target funerals knowing there would be many people gathered; consequently, the damage would be greater. My sister-in-law's life was shattered forever as she lost her dad, lost without a trace because he was in a place where a suicide bomber chose to claim his victims. There was nothing left of him, which his family could identify and place in his coffin with dignity. He was denied the right to be buried in love, respect and worth, which so rightfully was his. The family ended up having his suit in the coffin, an empty suit with an invisible body. A truly noble man, full of life, with so much grandeur and grace, had done nothing wrong to anybody, worked so hard to raise his family, ended up literally disappearing from the face of the earth for no fault of his own. Man's doing! Go and ask his family, if you dare, what do they think about war? No closure, no proper grieving, of course, only millions of why? When tears don't do; when words are no more; when screams are tearing the inside of you; when nothing is sacred; when life is gone forever, no goodbyes, only injustice and eternal loss. What can you say to mind-numbing evil beings terrorising the neighbourhood and destroying life, turning humans to dust? What do you say to those who created this mess?

Today, it is all beyond repair. Have we crossed the point of no return? Where I live, we moan and groan when driving over a pothole that keeps appearing randomly with every change of weather. This was not the cause of the damage to the roads in Iraq, of course. The roads were destroyed by army tanks parading in the streets during the invasion and the toppling of the then the ruling regime. The naive ordinary people celebrated, thinking they were bringing peace and stability. How could tanks be allowed to move on the weak roads? Roads that were already wrecked by the bombings and explosions. Now completely destroyed by the weight of these tanks. Today, these roads are still waiting to be repaired.

Millions of people were denied basic needs, no electricity, no water, no food, surviving in the most primitive way; mixing sawdust with flour to increase its amount so there would be enough bread for the whole family to eat. This was a reality for thousands of families. The two great rivers were turned into puddles under the watching eye of other countries and the United Nations; no one blinked an eye. Would you blame this on God just like we blame Him for every other mess humans create?

A ruling evil power was replaced by another ruling evil power, and the outside world took sides. The worlds' superpowers took opposite sides. Here is my memory of the ongoing war in Iraq, nearly forty years of human suffering: during the Iran\Iraq war and whenever there was a battle on the war front, families would be holding their breath when spotting a fleet of taxis with boxes on top heading to the wretched households. These boxes bore precious cargos, the coffins of soldiers who lost their lives in the trenches, so alone and so worthless. They would have the flag of the country wrapped around the box, secured on top of a taxi, and sent to their parents. When you see these taxis, you would wonder 'is that taxi heading to my street? Is it going to stop in front of my house? Is my brother's dead body in that box?' All men were forced to be soldiers, everybody from age 18–45, so every family was hit. When a family was cursed by losing their son, in such a meaningless way, a black rectangular piece of cloth, a metre wide and probably eighty centimetres long, would be hung outside the house. It would get secured high up on the front wall of the house so every passer-by could see. A scene to behold, marking the loss of a son, referred to as a martyr. Written on the black cloth, in white colour, would be the name of the worthless young man, whose life was so cheap and wasted, the day when he was killed and the battle location. To the shame of every human being who had anything or any involvement in the war, I have seen a house with six of these black clothes hanged outside the front wall of the same house: six black clothes, one for each of their six sons. The last black cloth, which looked fresh and new compared to the other five older ones, read: 'Their sixth and last son.' This was a reality which my eyes have seen. This is man's doing. Humans without the love and the fear of God. Why? I was only a passer-by, yet the scene has scarred me for life. Does anybody even remember these young six brothers? Can you imagine if you were that parent? What existence were they forced to endure? Years of war and fighting, what for? And why? Here is the irony, please, my reader, I need you to focus, the lives of the six brothers sacrificed for defending their country Iraq against the enemy Iran; today, many of the Iraqi ruling officials had fought against the Iraqi army, against the six brothers. I am not sure what the six brothers' mother would make of this if alive! Man's depravity at its worst. What did she lose her six sons for? Life is a sick, sad and wicked joke. Total destruction caused by man's evil mind and man's doing.

Man's Harvest

Enduring war, not to mention the assault by the so-called Islamic State and the ongoing sectarian civil war, I will be forgiven to pause the questions where is love? Where is forgiveness? The evil spirit is rife, ruling our world, making one person the enemy of another. Many will not stop and ponder; instead, we find it easier to blame it on God. When we tell lies as part of our daily existence, when all we can utter are words of hatred and demeaning to other people, when we can't stand the sight of each other, when we steal someone's else possession, when we envy the car or the house of another person, when it upsets us to think other children do better than our children, when it makes us feel good to see other people fail, when we cause others to be reduced to nothing, curled up in a corner, their eyes burning with silent tears, when our pride makes us walk like a balloon which is about to burst, when we behave like everybody else is beneath us because our bank account is loaded with money, when our designer clothes are so much more expensive than anyone else's. Multiply this by thousands and thousands of times, and you get a much graver impact, and this is when countries treat each other as enemies.

When the wealth of this earth is wasted on fighting each other, and when peace is a word which some celebrities occasionally choose for publicity. When I do not like you because you do not have the same skin colour as mine and when your shed blood is cheap because it is not my blood, blame it all on God, why don't you?

God gifted us with free will. Sadly, the free will of man, influenced by evil desires and greed has brought about an endless river of death and destruction. Hatred has replaced love. Revenge has replaced forgiveness. People have committed so much evil against each other that your ears would refuse to hear it, let alone believe it. Dogs were seen scavenging on parts of human bodies, left in the streets, bodies which were not cleared by the state and not claimed by relatives. If every sadness inflicted on me had left a hole in my body, then what you would see of me today would be a ghost, an outline of a person. I have seen what happens when a man chooses evil's way and roam the streets like lords and kings.

Who is making the decisions of war? Who is planning where the next war should be? Who agrees to it? Who turns a blind eye? Which countries attend meetings in the name of peace? Who executes these decisions? Who provides the weapon? Who makes the weapon? Who sells the weapon? God gave us brains; we should know what is right and what is wrong. Stop and ask what do you think this weapon will do? Defend you if attacked? So why sell it?

Neighbour against neighbour and everybody against Christians. In the year 1968, people from the Gulf countries, including the United Arab Emirates, would travel to Iraq in order to use the Iraqi airlines to travel aboard. How can a nation change from well-educated, generous, and decent citizens into monsters who live on taking lives? A country that is so rich in its natural resources that a whole continent could live on the money it could generate. How can a whole generation be transformed from human beings into rejects, fighting internally, killing each other? Years of suffering and years of war for what?

Destruction is the absence of God. Greed, filth and hatred rule where God is not present. Watch man's harvest all around you, and I dare you not to be moved.

God Overrules

Do not ask where God is? Instead, ask where love is? Why would people choose hatred and revenge over love and forgiveness? Do not ask where God is. Ask why man is allowed to destroy that which God created? Why not use the creative minds God gave us to build?

As a Christian, I accept that evil rules our world, but I believe God overrules. You might ask, my reader, 'If God exists, why does He not stop evil?' As humans, we are gifted with the gift of love. God, in His majesty, placed an ingredient in every human heart to be able to love. With love, we can transform life on earth, and we can create heaven on earth if only we love one other. God also has gifted us with a second important ingredient, which is the freedom of the will. We are free to love and express our love to people living around us, to situations we face, and to our decisions making. What if every person and every government on our planet chose, through the freedom of the will, to express the sentiment and the reality of love? I think the question then should be changed to 'Why doesn't mankind stop evil?' instead of asking 'why doesn't God stop evil?' We are created with heart and brain capable of choosing to love rather than to hate, build rather than destroy, live in peace rather than with war. My neighbour's two daughters, two young lives were destroyed by a shotgun triggered by their brother. If there were love and forgiveness in my neighbour' household, no evil cloud would have engulfed the family and turned their existence into misery. If there was love in Iraq, I would still have my home.

My prayer is to you, my reader, that God in His majesty, will reach out to you and protect you from being swamped by today's thinking, which is influenced by evil intent, deceived by the glitz and glamor of the media and the populous stand. I am not a narcissistic individual who think God, this omnipotent almighty one, has nothing else better to do but to sort my finances for me, guide me through my life with Ray, speak to me through a little sparrow, find me the best job, sort my brother's future, give me three amazing girls, granting me my heart's desire every time I prayed or sighed in silent prayer. I believe none of what happened to me since my childhood was a coincidence, or by chance or luck. Every step I took, I am persuaded it was planned and executed by my Maker and my Father because I believe. I accepted His free gift of faith. I trusted His wisdom. I made Him the centre of my life, the overseer, the guest of honour, the warmth which keeps me alive, the never-ending power supply, and my faithful companion. I consult Him in every little detail of my life. My God is interested in it all, and I know He is interested in every detail of your life, my reader. Don't let anyone else tell you otherwise.

Chapter 24

My Reader

And then He showed up, Wednesday 20/2/2019

As I was driving to work this morning, I was listening to the words of a worship song: "Worthy, You are worthy, King of kings Lord of lords, I worship you…" I decided I am to put on paper the times my God showed up in my life when I desperately needed a lifeline.

If we were to accept history, if we were to believe characters who lived in past centuries existed, then we are to accept the Lord Jesus exited too. He lived not because the Bible tells us so but because umpteen other historic documents, sights and facts confirm his life on earth. People with no faith and people from other faiths would agree that Jesus was a good man. His teaching surpassed any other teaching; His statements have defied time and space. Two things I would share with you, my reader, here is one of Jesus's teachings from the book of Mark, 12:30–31, New International Version (NIV).

"Love the Lord your God with all your heart and with all your soul and with all your mind and with all your strength.' The second is this: 'Love your neighbour as yourself.' There is no commandment greater than these."

What if everybody followed this profound teaching, including the government's civil servants, the local governments, business owners, the bankers, the social media workers, and users. More importantly, the politicians and the decision-makers, and those involved in making weapons and those who choose war and destruction? Imagine what life would have been if mankind applied one of Jesus's teachings. Iraq would've been the beautiful garden that God planned it to be. There would have been no pain and misery, no bloodshed, no immigrants, no lost homes, no discrimination, no hatred, no revenge, no weapons and no wars. If only we applied Jesus' teaching to love one another.

Would you agree with me, my reader, and I bet many psychiatrists would agree that nothing cleanses the soul and heals wounds like forgiveness. Many broken hearts will mend, many relationships will be restored, and many mental health issues will be resolved if only we forgave one other. When Jesus was asked about forgiveness, His answer was we should forgive each other from our heart, not seven times but seventy-seven times (Matthew 18:22). What if the divine gifts of love and forgiveness were to enter every human heart, and with our free will, we all lived accordingly? What if?

And if you are not sure, my reader, about the existence of God, then please consider these lines which I picked for you from the book of Romans 1:20. 'For since the creation of the world God's invisible qualities – His eternal power and divine nature – have been clearly seen, being understood from what has been made, so that men are without excuse.'

Why don't you have another look at the beautiful nature around you, pay attention to the four seasons, the oceans, the universe, every system in the human body, every detail of any flower you want to pick, any animal or bird you want to study, the life which took place before you were born, and the life after when you are gone. God, in His majesty, the maker of heaven and earth, the amazing power of love, chose to come down on earth, down to our level and took the body of a person and became a man called Jesus, all because God is love. God loves you, and God loves me. God reached out to you and me in the person of Jesus to teach us about love and forgiveness and many more amazing qualities. The Designer knows its design inside out. Why not trust the wisdom of the maker?

What does every heart crave for? What is the solution to every problem in the world? What could have avoided past catastrophes? What could eliminate and remove any devastation in the world? What could heal every broken heart? What could be the answer to every need? How could we have a better world? How many young people's lives could be spared from depression, anxiety and the rising of mental health issues? Simply put, by love and forgiveness. So, what is the message of the Gospel? What did Jesus's good news proclaim? You guessed it: love and forgiveness.

There is the ultimate forgiveness, one with immeasurable magnitude, the one we can claim through the Cross. Jesus, on His death and resurrection, built a bridge to lead us to our heavenly Father. By His death on the cross, forgiveness was displayed and granted. So, if every bad word ever said against another person, every dark and evil thought we had, every time someone cheated, every horrible decision was made against an innocent person, every time life or a family was destroyed, every badness ever committed since the start of time and till the end of time, all of them will be wiped away. All forgiven, and all forgotten, because the price for all this has been paid on the Cross. All at hand, through faith and ask for forgiveness. Only then a new creation will be born in each one of us. Repent and believe and let your Heavenly Father guide your steps. My job is not to convince you, my reader, about the Good News of the Gospel. I am not burdened to bring lost souls to God. It is not my doing to argue the case for God. But in my humble and simple way, I shared with you the love God lavished upon me, how my God showed up every time I cried out to Him, and the difference His presence had in my life. God knows His children. God is supernatural. The natural man cannot discern the things of God. I believe God comes to His children in different ways. If God is speaking to your heart, if God is making you willing to call upon Him, then please, I urge you, do not miss His call. This could be your moment. Do not ignore it. When you meet Him, all your questions will fade away. Although none of His children will be lost, however, sadly not everyone will be called. Jesus promised He would build His church, brick by brick, that is you and me and all the other believers. Jesus is the foundation of His church. You, and I, my reader, are God's inheritance. In this world, people are letting the evil spirit run their lives and controlling their minds. As for me, I believe the battle belongs to the Lord, the almighty, and the victory was sealed on the Cross.

If you are old or young, if you have a few hours left on this plant, or if you are a young person, I am praying for you, my reader, as I am writing these lines. And if you are blessed to be a perfect person who has never done any wrong in your life, perhaps occasionally a little white lie now and then. Your character traits have equipped you with what you need to overcome life's troubles, and you have successfully achieved your goals, then good on you. But being a great human being, and stop there, you will end up a tiny little dust left behind. You are no more, gone for eternity. I am convinced God is looking for His own, watching them, and chasing them. In His time, He will call them. There is a verse in the Bible that says, 'You will seek me and find me when you seek me with all your heart.' (Jeremiah 29:13)

To become a child of God, born from above. It is like having another birth, becoming a brand-new person, clean from inside and out – the start of a relationship between you and heaven.

As we are nearing the end, here is a wee treat for you, my reader. It is the words of the Lord's Prayer in Aramaic, the old Aramaic. It is the closest to how it would have sounded when the Lord Jesus said it when He taught his disciples how to pray:

Awan (our father) deshamia (in heaven) nethqadash (hallowed be) shmakh (your name) teethy malkoothakh (your kingdom come) Nehwey soyankh (you will be done) aykana deshmaya (as it is in heaven) ab baraa (also on earth) halan lakhma semquanan youmana (gives us this day our daily bread) wshwaqulan hawbane wahetahane (forgive us our debts) aikanan da behnan shoqulan hayawane (as we forgive our debters) latalan nisyouna ila pisa min bisha (lead us not into temptation, but deliver us from evil) matool ilakhy malkootha (yours is the kingdom) wa hayla wa toshbohta (the power and the glory) elalam almeen ameen (now and forever amen).

Chapter 25
Final Words

Today, my three girls have their own lives, facing up to their own responsibilities and following their own path. Their sharp minds and kind hearts filled with empathy for those around them will lead them through life's encounters. Each will have her own story to tell. Will they be the parents of the fourth generation living in a fourth country? Who knows? I pray I will be around when my girls call upon me when bringing a new life to this world. I have promised myself to be at their bidding. I wait in anticipation for every new change and a new story they content with. I constantly pray for His presence in my girls' lives. My parents had seven children and eighteen grandchildren. I am not sure how many little ones Ray will be "babbi sawa" for. My future services are already booked for when I retire. I know Ray will be a super grandpa with his amazing dance moves, the best Maths tutor, and new episodes of sharky and barky and detective Mason are waiting to be told. Soon, the fox family will pack their bags and will be busy digging holes in someone else's back garden.

Since I was eighteen years old, I have been made to associate Iraq with a land crippled with an unending war and suffering, yet I was always hopeful, longing for it to be redeemed one day. However, watching the news on television one day, fields of wheat and barley scorched by deliberate fires, ruined in a scale never seen before, made me wonder what next? Any hope of redemption was burnt in those fires. I woke up one day, and I decided I am selling my parents' house. It was the tenth anniversary of my mother's passing. I came to the conclusion that none of my siblings will ever go back to Iraq. It was time to cut any ties with our past. I contacted my siblings, and with a heavy heart, they all agreed. Little we knew this would become a very lengthy and painful process. We faced huge hurdles every step of the way.

My parents' house was finally sold. We probably got a third of its worth. My siblings and I pondered upon my parents' lives and our fond memories of two amazing parents. We each received our share of what our parents considered their eighth child. Each one of us on our own, in the country we live in, thousands of miles away from each other. We have nothing left in that land, our birthplace but not our home anymore. Nothing to connect us to it, except our parents' bones, thousands of miles away, lost and scattered like our memories of when we were there, many years ago.

The End